NE 7/10/22

THE
WALL

THE
WALL

SMASH SELF-DOUBT AND BECOME THE TRUE YOU

ANT MIDDLETON

HarperCollins*Publishers*

HarperCollins*Publishers*
1 London Bridge Street
London SE1 9GF

www.harpercollins.co.uk

HarperCollins*Publishers*
1st Floor, Watermarque Building, Ringsend Road
Dublin 4, Ireland

First published by HarperCollins 2022

1 3 5 7 9 10 8 6 4 2

© Ant Middleton 2022

Ant Middleton asserts the moral right to
be identified as the author of this work

A catalogue record of this book is
available from the British Library

HB ISBN 978-0-00-847235-1
PB ISBN 978-0-00-847236-8

Printed and bound in the UK using 100%
renewable electricity at CPI Group (UK) Ltd

To my cousin George.
Keep flying high, knowing that you're in a
place where you belong and where no
judgement is passed!

CONTENTS

YOU FEEL STUCK IN YOUR LIFE

THE WALL. SOONER or later we all hit it. The wall might be anything. It might be your lack of motivation, it might be that you have no self-belief, it might be your fear of leaving your comfort zone, it might be that you're struggling to get over the loss of a loved one, it might be that you spend too much time with people who undermine you, or it might be a relationship that you need to get out of.

What all these things have in common is that they're holding you back. They're the things that seem as if they're stopping you from reaching your true potential, from getting the most you can out of your life.

That's where this book comes in. I want to share with you my strategies and techniques for smashing through the things that are standing between you and the best version of yourself.

One of the most amazing things about what I do these days is the interactions I have with people from every walk of life. I get to talk to them about what they're going through. Sometimes I'm even able to help them. I feel brilliant and really lucky when that happens.

People turn to me because I think differently. I give them different ways of looking at the world and their own place in it. They know that I'm not happy to accept the norm quietly if the norm doesn't work. I'm not interested in the generic, in the off-the-peg. Whatever it is I'm faced by, I want to work out the solution for myself.

They also know that I can speak from experience. My failure to fully confront the fact of my father's death held me back for years. It left me lost in the void; I sabotaged my life over and over again. I've experienced this in my working life too. Because I'm obsessed with what I do, I hit a wall every five or six years. At the beginning of a new project, I'm full of energy and drive, and I push and push until I'm operating at the upper limit of what I'm capable of. And then, at some point, all the positivity starts to give way to resentment and frustration. I snap at people and feel angry without every really understanding why.

The wall!

In those cases, the wall becomes something I just need to get rid of. Once it's been brought down, I can then feel all the tension that's been building up inside me flood away. I breathe easier, my enthusiasm returns. It's like getting a second wind.

And that's the thing. Hitting the wall isn't as bad as it appears at first. Yes, it feels frustrating and uncomfortable, but it's a sign that you've already evolved to the point where you've outgrown your current circumstances. The person you're with in that relationship isn't moving with you anymore. You feel stagnant in your career because it no longer challenges you. You're not happy with your body and want to lose weight. You hate the fact that you can't seem to make decisions. You want to change but you can't break old habits.

Life is all about finding out who you are, where you fit in. You'll hit many walls along the way. The truth is, sometimes you'll outgrow people and places and jobs.

So, if you're angry with yourself because you struggle to find motivation, then good! This is a positive outcome. You've recognised something about yourself that needs to change if you're to keep moving forward in your life. Your frustration at discovering that you can't motivate yourself is also the first step towards grabbing that momentum.

Deep down, you know that you can do better than this. You know that you need to change, that you need to do things differently, go in a different direction. You need to focus on yourself. The friction is just a sign that while the situation you're in at the moment might be about to end, something new is ready to start.

This is where you get to make a choice. Either you complain about how stuck you feel and sit there, hoping someone or something will change things for you. Or you realise that it's up to you, and only you, to get through it.

* * *

I HOPE THAT this book is something you'll be able to draw on as you go on that journey. *The Wall* is going to be a bit different to my previous books. As always, it'll contain hard-won lessons from my own life. But there will also be examples taken from my encounters with people who I like to think I've helped. I'm so inspired by seeing their resilience and strength, their own iron-clad determination to overcome tough times and challenges.

There will be activities and exercises for reflection to help you really absorb and engage with the ideas contained within these pages. This is the first time I've done anything like this in my adult books and you'll find them scattered through the text. I've included them because I want you to see *The Wall* as a collaboration between me and you. Every single reader will see the same words, but every single reader will also make something different of them. A book is a brilliant start, but that's all it is. It's a jumping-off point. You've got to go out there and discover what works in *your* life. Make every idea in here your own. Break things. Make mistakes. Find out who you really are.

Because until you do that, there will always be a wall standing in your way.

CHAPTER 1

YOU'RE AFRAID OF WHAT OTHERS THINK OF YOU

I ONCE READ something that has stuck with me ever since. A flea can jump approximately 300 times its height. If you put a flea into a closed box, it will carry on jumping. For the first fifteen or twenty times it will try to propel itself into the air as high as it possibly can. And every time the poor creature will smash into the box's lid. After that it will learn. From then on, its jumps will be perfectly calibrated to *just* skim the top of its new home.

What I find saddest is that if, after a certain amount of time has elapsed, you set that flea free, it will carry on jumping as if it's still in the box. This always comes to mind when I think about ways in which our desire to please and to conform can become a massive obstacle on our way to achieving our true potential. Too many of us are far too worried about what other human beings think or say about us. It's paralysing. And to a certain extent that's not surprising. Those in power, society, negative people all want to suppress us. All of them are threatened by our freedom. So they force us to act like those fleas.

Society has rules. And they are necessary. Without laws we'd all be existing in a state of chaos. But those rules can be overly restrictive, even asphyxiating. We're constantly being told that we should be grateful for the job that we have, that we're lucky to even be in a relationship, that we should mindlessly repeat whatever opinions are deemed appropriate at any given moment. Why rock the boat? we're asked. Why cause unnecessary trouble? Well, sod that. It's all just a construct.

There are days when I feel as if my life is a constant struggle against the expectations that others are trying to force onto me. Most of the time, the direction my energy is pointing me in is in tension with what others want me to do. But I'll always back the messages *my* body and mind are giving me. Why would I want to let other human beings define my limits? I'm my own person, with my own values, and I'm not ashamed of that.

The fact is, though, that most people don't think for themselves. It's easier to just go along with the crowd. And it's because of this, because most people know deep down that they've surrendered control of their lives, that they *hate* it when they come across somebody who has chosen to be free. They see this person's freedom as a criticism. How wrong is that? When has any good ever come from setting your bar only as high as the lowest common denominator?

The thing that astonishes me is that although there is a whole fucking lot of pressure being placed on every single one of us, ultimately, we're the ones who are brainwashing ourselves. We're doing their work for them. We become our own secret police, monitoring ourselves, repressing any sign of individuality, because we're worried about what others might say or think if we showed them who we really are.

All of this means that the thought of being judged, or laughed at, or condemned, or even pitied is a huge wall for so many of us. It's one of the biggest things stopping so many people from becoming the best versions of themselves. It limits people, forces them to spend too much of their time on this planet living in cramped boxes. Perhaps that has always been true, but the current atmosphere in society and the rise of social media have magnified that trait in us. The sad fact is that people talk, and negativity sells.

And it's not just that this terror of being judged limits your horizons. When we allow what others do and say to affect the way we feel, it floods our body with stress. All of the negativity we experience from others finds a home in our bodies. So, if your happiness and sense of self-worth depend on what other people say and do, then you'll always be caught in the same painful trap.

But here's the good news. It's precisely the fact that we've become our own persecutors that means we can also be our own liberators. There's no secret solution, no potion you can drink that can make you immune or stop you caring. The answer is much more straightforward, even if to begin with it might seem harder: be true to yourself. A lot of shit will come your way, but if you stay true to who you are, then you'll never get lost or confused or side-tracked.

To do that, you have to be willing to make uncomfortable decisions without giving a fuck what anybody else says. You have to realise that it's *all* about you. Often this means going against what's expected of you. Are you willing to say no? Are you willing to upset people? Are you willing to focus on yourself and ignore others? Are you willing to take the backlash? Are you willing to stick at it even when times are hard? Are you willing to accept that in order to get to where you need to be, you're going to experience serious discomfort?

Good. Let's get going.

YOUR INTEGRITY IS NOT A COMMODITY

If you're the sort of person who flip-flops all over the place, who shifts their opinion to match whatever's the fashionable thing to believe on any given day, then how can people ever trust you? How can they rely on you? Why would they ever be interested in a single thing you think or say?

Fakeness, inauthenticity, confusion. They're the penalties you pay for being a people-pleaser, because other human beings can see through those performances. These deceptions and compromises might be able to work for a little while, but there's no disguise that you can put on that will work for ever.

People go along with all sorts of things that they don't agree with because they want to get paid, or because they want to be liked, or because they think it will bring them greater opportunities. But the biggest reward, the thing that money can't buy, is being true to who you are. There's no price on that. A pound earned by being faithful to who you are and what you believe in is easily worth a hundred pounds earned by pretending to be a person you're not.

You need to remember that it doesn't matter if other people criticise you; what's important is that you shouldn't end up hating yourself because you've suppressed your personality or beliefs or ambitions in an attempt to become the sort of person you think others want you to be.

What matters most isn't how others see you, it's how you see yourself. Be true to yourself. Never, ever feel ashamed of who you really are. But, as always, honesty is important here. Ask yourself: What are my foundations? What are my values? What matters most to me? Then make sure you enact those things in your day-to-day life. Hold tight to them, don't let anyone ever persuade you to relinquish them. All of this is work that is worth doing, because when you're sure of who you are, it becomes a lot easier to ignore the shit other people throw in your direction.

I know who I am. I know what I'm worth. I know that I'm a good person. I'll never pretend to be someone I'm not. I stand up for what I believe in, I keep my integrity. Because my integrity is the part of me that's most precious. It's something that cannot be bought or sold. That's why when people feel as if they can take a pop at me in the press, I'm not going to bother replying. I just let it wash over me.

THEIR PROBLEM, NOT YOURS

It's so easy to get obsessed by the idea of what someone else thinks of you. Very often it leads to you working out ways in which you can squash yourself, your personality and your needs so that this person will like you more, or respect or applaud you – even just behave a bit more kindly towards you.

But what you should never forget is that whatever they think about you is the product of their own experiences, prejudices and insecurities. It has almost nothing to do with who you actually are. They don't know you – not the real you. And they don't know what you're going through. Whatever they might say to you, whatever criticism they toss in your direction, says much more about them than about you. When you realise that, then it begins to seem irrational to care about what they think.

EXERCISE
HAVE AN OUT-OF-BODY EXPERIENCE

If you're always bending and twisting who you are to fit what you think other people want you to be, then you're going to run the risk of becoming lost. After a while, you won't really know who you are.

You'll think that the carefully curated, anxiously constructed version of yourself that you present to the world is the only way you'll ever receive the love and praise you're so desperate for.

Why is it that you want that love and praise? When you realise that none of this is important, and that you'll never actually get the love and praise that you crave, then you'll realise that distorting who you really are in an attempt to secure it is a dead end. It's an illusion, like those guys in history who spent their days trying to turn lead into gold.

Take a step back. Imagine that you're watching somebody else put a mask on every time they meet somebody new. What would you say to them?

THE ONLY OPINION THAT MATTERS

If you want to cut out those negative voices, then the first thing to do is to remind yourself that the only person on the whole planet whose opinion matters is you. Why on earth would you ever let what anybody else might think stop you from making the most of your existence?

I met Danny at a signing for my last book. He was a really nice young lad, bursting with enthusiasm, but shy. So shy that he could barely return my gaze. Instead, he hid beneath the thatch of thick brown hair that crept down over his eyes. He was obsessed with music, he told me. It's all he thought about from the moment he woke up till the moment his head hit the pillow at night. He was an electrician, but what he really wanted to do was be in a band. He wrote songs in his bedroom, he said, and there was part of him that was desperate to take them out into the world to find out if he had any chance of making it. The problem, he explained, was that he was shit-scared of what his mates would say.

'I'm worried they'll laugh at me, or take the piss,' he said, his voice faltering. 'I'm a bit different from them. I'm not sure they really understand me, and I think if I get up on stage and make a tit of myself they'll never let me forget it.'

'But why would you ever want other people's opinions to be the barrier that stops you from finding out the limits of your potential?' I replied. 'That's something you should discover for yourself. If you stay in the box they've built for you, you'll live with regret for the rest of your life. That regret will eat you up. And for what? Something very important to you will have been squashed. Now, ask yourself, is it worth it just to make sure nobody criticises you, or laughs at you? Maybe you *are* a shit singer. Maybe when you get up on stage everyone *will* laugh and joke. But at least you'll know then, and you can laugh and joke along with them, and then move on with a new lesson under your belt. But imagine never giving yourself the chance to find out?'

What I was trying to explain to Danny is the same thing I always try to say to anyone else in his position: the people who give you shit and try to put you off trying to better yourself aren't going to have to live with the regret that will come if you decide to listen to them. But you will. Whatever it is that you're considering doing – whether that's changing careers or changing haircuts – you should be doing for you, and you alone. You're not doing it on behalf of your mates, or your parents, or your colleagues at work. You should be doing it to progress who *you* are, to get that bit closer to the best version of yourself, to increase your chances of living a happy and fulfilled life. If you think that the path you've chosen is right for you, then I promise you, that's all that matters. So, remind me, why should you care what anybody else thinks?

PUT ON YOUR ARMOUR

I know that sometimes what I do is misunderstood. Sometimes people will talk about me. I'm fine with that. It shows me that what I'm doing is new and different. People don't like the unfamiliar or the unconventional. It threatens them. So when they see you behaving in that way, they try to suppress those traits in you.

You should never feel as if you have to bow to that peer pressure. You have nothing to apologise for. But don't fool yourself that it's going to be easy. Be prepared to be misunderstood. Be prepared to take the shit. Be prepared to be badmouthed.

A portion of this process is just realising that, in all likelihood, the people whose opinion you're worried about are the sorts of human beings who are trying to drag you down because they can't get up to your level. As soon as anybody shows a spark of talent, or bravery, or ambition, they move as quickly as they can to stamp it out. There's no reason in the entire world to worry yourself about what someone as jealous, as ignorant and as afraid as that would say. It's more about them than it is about you.

The other portion of the process is about being a bit more proactive about protecting yourself. It's bloody easy for me to just say, 'Shut those voices out.' I know it's never quite as simple as that. And yet, as I explained to Danny, you can put your armour on in advance.

'If you're worried that your friend Mike is going to tell you you're a wanker for getting up on stage then, guess what, in a sense the worst has already happened. You've already heard him say that to you in your head and you've survived it. The bullet has ricocheted off your armour. So what are you afraid of?'

That's what I did when I was struggling in the early days in the military. I knew that I'd get shit for being a bit smaller than some of the other soldiers: 'Ant, you need to bulk up – you're only nine stone and you're carrying half your weight. What the fuck do you think you're doing? Just give up.'

I was honest with myself. I worked out which part of that I needed to listen to (the constructive criticism) and which bit I needed to ignore (everything else). It meant that as soon as the sergeant major opened his mouth, I was prepared. I knew how to protect myself. It's a progressive mindset rather than a reactive one.

Danny needed to do the same thing. Was he worried about criticism because he knew that some of his lyrics needed polishing or his guitar-playing needed to be improved? Or was he worried about people behaving like negative twats because they've got nothing better to do with their lives than try to shrink somebody else's existence?

His response to this was really telling. For the first time in our whole conversation he stared back directly into my eyes. 'No,' he said, 'I'm ready to go. I just … I'm just scared of looking like an idiot. I'm scared of people thinking I'm getting above myself.'

'Are you getting above yourself?'

'No.'

'Is what you're doing insulting anybody? Is what you're doing hurting anybody?'

'No!' He looked surprised when I asked this.

'Exactly. So they have no right to judge you. What they say or do does not fucking matter one iota. Spend time now imagining the worst of what they could say. None of it matters, does it? None of it is any reflection on you or your abilities? The only person it reflects badly on is them.'

That seemed to hit home. He mumbled a thank you and walked off into the night. I didn't expect to hear from him again, but a couple of months later he sent me a message on Instagram to say that he'd played at a couple of open-mic nights in the city he lived in. He wasn't sure whether this was going to turn into anything more meaningful, but he was glad that he'd found the courage to at least give it a go. For too long he'd let his fears about what other people might say about him define his existence. By getting up and doing what he did, he was defining himself.

Hearing that made my day.

WHEN YOU DO this work of preparing yourself, you'll learn a whole load more about yourself, and crucially you'll have learned a bit more about how to manage your emotions (see Chapter 10 on p. 172 for more on this). You've looked at that negative situation that promised to work against you, and turned it into a positive situation that has the potential to work for you.

Because, as I see it, you're not filling your head with reasons to stop, you're filling it with the ammunition that will help you succeed. Use that time wisely before you make the commitment. Think about your strengths and weaknesses. Identify the stuff that you know will be able to slide through your armour and really get to you. Why is it that you're particularly worried about what that particular person will say? When you've worked that out then you can just bat it to one side and use it as inspiration. 'You think that? Well, I'll fucking show you how wrong you are.' You can turn their weapons against them.

SET BOUNDARIES

So far I've talked about the way that the fear of what those around us will think stops us from doing the things we want to do. But that same fear can also work the other way round – it can make us do things we don't want to do. People-pleasers agree to do things for others even when they know it will make them less happy and more stressed. They do this because they're so terrified of how the other people might react. What they don't realise is that if they're willing to set a few boundaries, then not only will they save themselves that anxiety, they will actually be more respected as a result.

I'm always being asked for favours by other people. Can you come to this? Can you endorse that? If I can help, I do. Most of the time, though, I just can't. I'm not going to tear myself to pieces to make other people's lives a tiny bit easier. And I'm not going to sacrifice spending time with human beings I love for the sake of someone I've never met. So as clearly, firmly and politely as I can, I tell them what they're asking isn't possible. Be honest. Never tell a white lie – you'll just end up feeling shit about having done so and will probably end up laying a trap that you'll fall into further down the line.

I guarantee that most people will react far better than you expect. In fact, they'll respect you all the more for being so upfront and clear. But if they do give you a hard time, then you'll have got all the proof you need that you should never have got involved with them in the first place.

LESSONS

- Don't throw away the best parts of you because you're listening to what the worst parts of the world have to say. Only one person's opinion matters: yours.

- Hold on tightly to your integrity and your values. If you make sure that they're your foundation, you'll find it a lot easier to shrug off any criticism that comes your way.

- Don't suppress who you are because of what is, at the end of the day, nothing more than external noise. Try to filter it out, just as you would filter out the racket made by the bulldozers tearing up the street outside.

- If you've prepared yourself mentally for the sort of nonsense that's going to come your way, then it'll be easier to face if and when it does show up. You can take everything negative that's thrown at you, and use it as motivation.

- Don't be afraid of saying no. If you set clear boundaries, people won't be offended, but they will respect you more.

CHAPTER 2

YOU'RE SURROUNDING YOURSELF WITH THE WRONG PEOPLE

FOR THE FIRST time since we'd landed I took the chance to catch my breath, arrange my thoughts. I suddenly noticed how cold the night air was against my chin. *Almost time to go*, I told myself. I could see that the rest of my team had nearly caught up. My rifle was snug and firm in my arms. I'd trained and fought with it so much that it always felt to me like an extension of my own arm. I could throw it around with the same control and precision as a juggler exerts over his balls. *Almost time to go.* It was as if I was trying to force myself to make that move.

I tensed my muscles, readying them to thrust forward. Just as I was about to make that breach, another volley of bullets came through the door. Fucking hell. I snapped back to the position I'd just been in. Another pulse of adrenaline. I could feel it jangling through my body. This was strange. What was happening? In an attempt to restore my composure I told myself, *I've been here before. I've done this before. All I need to do is wait for the pause.*

The enemy always had their AK-47s on automatic. We'd been taught that you only need one, maybe two bullets to do the job. They preferred to spray the room. If someone has their gun on automatic, I knew they were panicking. If they were panicking, they were probably not that well trained. If they were not that well trained, then they were not going to know that when they fired on automatic, the weapon's muzzle got jerked up and they could only bring it down again by taking their finger off the trigger.

That gave you a pause of maybe a second and a half. Not long, but enough.

Wait for the pause. Wait for the pause. Then it came. I tried to move. Nothing. It was as if every limb in my body was paralysed. The connection between my body and mind was broken. The next moment bullets came slashing through the door, sending splinters flying in every direction, so many that before long it was beginning to look like a piece of lace.

I went to move again. I had to move again. Fuck! I slammed my body back against the wall. More bullets came. Another burst. I thought to myself, *Ant, wait for the pause.* Again, I made the calculation in my head. *All you need is a split second. I was hunting him. He's shit-scared. I'm better trained than him. I've got every advantage. Why can't I move? It's fear. What the fuck. What the fuck! How has this happened?* I tried to move my feet, but they remained rooted to the ground.

It was at that moment that I felt a gentle touch on my shoulder. It was one of my pals. He'd reached over and squeezed my shoulder twice, really softly. I knew he was telling me, *Don't worry, Ant. It's OK. I know what you're going through. The moment you go through that door, I'm going to be right behind you.* It was almost like an out-of-body experience. As soon as I felt the pressure on my shoulder, the anxiety and fear left me. Suddenly I felt invincible. I waited for the next burst of bullets, the next pause. And then, BANG!, I was straight in.

MOMENTS LIKE THAT underline the importance of having the right people around you. When I was struggling, when I could feel my nerve failing, a comrade stepped in to let me know that he was there for me; that he had my back. Knowing that gave me the courage I needed to do my job.

It's other people who help you smash through the wall. In fact, I'd go further. I believe that a life is only as good as the people who are in it. If you're hanging around with the wrong people, then nine times out of ten your life is going to be heading in the wrong direction.

You should surround yourself with positive people who benefit your life. They might be the sort of person you only have to sit with for a couple of minutes in order to start feeling better about yourself or so that your energy is restored. Or they might be the kind of friend who, when you're on the verge of doing something stupid to please someone that really doesn't deserve it, will give you the push you need to say no and stand up for yourself. Positive people will support and challenge you. Sometimes they'll do both at once.

Very often, I've found, what determines how tricky or not something feels isn't the scale of the task facing you, but the quality of the people around you at that moment in time. The single most important element of any project I get involved with is the people who are taking part in it. Sure, the idea has to be good, but there need to be trust and a sense of shared values. I've passed on brilliant-sounding opportunities because I haven't got the right vibe from the people I'd end up working with.

When you're around good people you feel more confident. Everything becomes more straightforward. Things that used to intimidate you, or that felt thorny and complex, lose the power they once had over you. You start to look forward to them. You feel comfortable expressing who you are, and know that you won't be judged if you fail.

The opposite is true when you're in a circle of negative human beings. Everything suffers: your confidence dissolves; you feel anxious and fearful; you struggle to trust others. That's why you should never be friends with people who are jealous of your success, or who want something from you, or who lie or talk shit about you behind your back. If you feel worse every time you see somebody, you should cut them out of your circle as soon as you can.

PRODUCT OF YOUR ENVIRONMENT

Do you know what happens when you surround yourself with good people? They will make you a better person. And, guess what, when you hang around with wasters, you'll become a waster too.

Do you want to be the sort of person who works during the week purely so you can get fucked-up at the weekend? Or do you want to be the sort of person who surrounds themselves with inspiring, talented, committed people. Think of all the practical and technical skills you can learn from them. But that's really just the start. When you're surrounded by people who value hard work, honesty and generosity, people who set high standards for themselves and expect others to match them, then that's the kind of behaviour that you'll try to display too. You'll want to emulate them.

Think of it as the best possible version of peer pressure. That was the atmosphere we had in the Special Forces. You didn't actually have to be the best of friends – with all those strong personalities that wasn't ever going to happen. But we all trusted and respected each other. When I sat in the helicopter on the way to a mission I'd look around at the lads and say to myself, 'I know you've bled, I know you've cried, I know you've suffered, I know you've pushed yourself to your limits and beyond to get where you are now.'

I never wanted to disappoint them. I never wanted for any of them to turn around, look at me and say to themselves: 'He doesn't belong here.' The standards there were ridiculous. If my performances dropped, you better believe they'd have let me know. We all relied on each other because our lives depended on it. It was such a stimulating, challenging environment to be in. It was humbling, but also inspiring. There was so much to learn from people who were experts in their field. We all fed off each other. Together, we felt unstoppable.

By contrast, there are over 100,000 people in the army, and they're all competing against each other – so much so, in fact, that it's a negative environment. It's Para Engineers against 7 RHA. Petty, pointless battles that are all about ego and very little to do with soldiering. That's why I was out within the year. Although, it should be said, not before I'd let peer pressure force me into drinking piss from an upturned desert boot. This is the absolute definition of an activity that doesn't benefit you as an individual in any way, shape or form. You're just doing it to fit in with a bunch of knobheads.

You don't need me to tell you that isn't the sort of atmosphere you should be cultivating.

* * *

I HAVE A great circle around me now. I know I can turn to them and be honest with them, and I know that they'll be honest with me. They're there for me when I need picking up, those times when it's felt as if the world is crashing down around me, and they're there to celebrate the good times. They give good advice when I need it; they're also not afraid to let me know when I'm behaving like a dick or wading into situations where I'll be painfully out of my depth. There were times, on Everest and in combat, where I exceeded the limits of what I was capable of. If somebody hadn't pulled me back, fuck knows what would have happened.

ALL FOR ONE AND ONE FOR ALL

I love Central London. Just driving through it excites me. But during the pandemic I paid it a visit, and for the first time that I can remember it didn't feel special or thrilling. It was a ghost town.

Then, a couple of weeks ago, I went back. There were people milling about in the streets. You could hear them laughing and arguing and shouting. Fuck me, I thought, *that's* what was missing. It's not the place, it's the people that make it mean something. It's difficult to find a life that feels meaningful if there aren't other human beings in it to share it with.

Shared experiences are so important, very often they're the bedrock of our happiness. And it's the networks of people we interact with in our life who give us the platform we need to thrive. You can't do everything yourself. That's just a fact.

When you really drill down, you realise that very few people's achievements are the result of one person working in complete isolation. There's always a team; there are always other human beings making contributions here and there. Sometimes they're big, sometimes they're small; but they're all crucial. Take just one piece away and the whole edifice might come crumbling down.

Steve Jobs was clearly a genius, a giant of our era. But his amazing achievements rested on the shoulders of incredible engineers and software developers as much as they did on his own insights and relentless drive.

Or consider bodybuilders. They might seem at first glance to be one of the ultimate examples of what a single individual can achieve, their successes built on a foundation of immense personal sacrifice and incredible dedication. But then think about the nutritionists who have given them advice on how to construct the perfect diet; think about their gym partners; think of the people at home who support them and give them the platform they need to go out and compete. They're enmeshed in a whole chain of other human beings' work.

None of this takes *anything at all* away from the body-builder themselves. And yet it's a valuable reminder that every individual accomplishment is also, in truth, a collective one. This shouldn't come as a surprise. Human beings are an inherently sociable species. Our survival, our position as the dominant creatures on this planet, rest in large part on our ability to form close connections with other human beings. Our success as a species has been built on our ancestors learning to trust each other, to co-operate, to watch each other's backs.

This is such an important thing to remember. Life is hard. Sometimes it can feel like an uphill struggle. But you don't have to tackle it alone. On those days when the wall before you seems insurmountable, you should never feel afraid of asking others for help.

HOW MANY PEOPLE DOES IT TAKE TO ... MAKE A DECISION?

Decision-making is another area of life that illustrates the importance of surrounding yourself with the right people. You need to know that whether you make the wrong call or the right call, your friends and family are still going to be there with you. If you're confident of that, it's far easier to take risks. You're more willing to step outside your comfort zone.

When you've got people by your side who you trust, who you know will understand when you fuck-up, then you're so much more likely to commit to riskier (or, to look at it another way, braver) options. Because you know that it won't be the end of the world if stuff goes wrong. We're all building each other up so that we're strong enough to survive anything.

If you don't have that then you don't make decisions. You don't commit to new things. Instead you stick to the basic, everyday shit that keeps you ticking along but that doesn't excite you. Your world won't grow.

My wife Emilie is a brilliant example of a supportive person who gives others the chance to go out there and take the steps they need to become the best version of themselves. As I've said before, the most important decision of your life, bar none, is who you partner up with. You need somebody compatible who understands you and accepts you for who you are. Somebody who pushes you to be the best version of yourself, not somebody who restricts you. When somebody truly loves you, they'll allow you to be yourself. I don't mean that they'll be a doormat, and in my eyes 'being yourself' is absolutely not going out on the lash with your mates every night of the week.

From the moment Emilie and I found each other I've thrived as an individual. I think she helped me find out who I really was, and that was so important. You need to know who you are before you can begin to believe in yourself. It was Emilie who'd always encourage me to follow my passions and dreams. More importantly, she gave me the platform I needed to find out what I was capable of. I didn't truly have self-belief until I met her.

Her message was always: 'If you think you might be able to do something, go out and do it.' So I did, and came back brimming with new-found confidence. She's always been happy to see me thriving, going to work happy.

Make sure you don't end up like those people who never achieve their potential because they're being held back by their partner. Find somebody who shares your values, who will be your strongest cheerleader, who gives you the support and space to become the best version of yourself. Find your Emilie.

TAKE A CHANCE ON ME

Who out there is going to enable you to succeed in the task you're about to embark on? More importantly, who is going to enable you to succeed as an individual?

In order to draw good people to you – and keep them there – you have to be willing to put your faith in them. They must believe that you believe in them.

Practice is always more important than theory. At the end of the day, the only way you'll know if you can trust some-one is to put your trust in them. How the hell are you ever going to know if you don't give them a chance?

Give them the opportunity to show that your instincts were correct!

Make sure that, in turn, you're that person who people know they can rely on. When your face floats into their mind, you want them to think: 'Yes, he's got my back.'

That was exactly how I approached every scenario in *Escape*. There's no way in the world we'd have had even the slimmest chance of getting out if I'd acted as if I knew everything myself and refused to put my trust in the other team members. They were all strangers. I knew nothing about them right up until the moment we were plonked into the middle of the desert or jungle or wherever. I'm not a mechanic. Me fiddling around with engines would have ended very badly. But I do know how to graft, and I do know how to manage people.

So I just kept it simple. What do you know? What can you bring to this situation? What don't you know? What *shouldn't* I ask you to do? Once we'd established all that, I gave everyone their head. I wanted them to see that I had faith in them so that they were inspired to repay that belief by doing the best job that they could.

If you can't trust others, you can't call yourself a leader.

WITH GREAT POWER COMES GREAT RESPONSIBILITY

You've got to bring something to the table. How can *you* benefit your team? How can *you* benefit your social circle? I don't mean money or a big house, I mean what is it about you and your personality that improves the lives of the people who come into contact with you?

Be the ally to others you'd want for yourself. When you're trying to think of how you can contribute to the lives of the people you have around you, try to think of the qualities you look for in other people and try to embody them yourself. If you're looking for loyalty, positivity and honesty, then try to make sure that you practise those values too. Think of yourself as your friends' and family's ally.

This attitude is essential when you're part of a team. Don't ever be a spare prick. If you can't see an immediate way to help others, don't hide away pretending to be busy, hoping that nobody asks you what the hell it is you're actually doing. I hate busy fools. Don't be that person who'd rather look important than actually want to contribute.

Why wouldn't you want to operate as close to your full potential as you possibly can? Why would you opt to pretend to be achieving things because you think it makes you look good, when you could actually be out there building stuff. You might be able to fool other people into giving you credit, but you can't ever fool yourself.

If you've got good people around you, make sure that they feel trusted and valued. If you're the kind of boss who treats your best employees like shit and constantly ignores their requests for a raise, don't be surprised if they walk out of the door. If you're the sort of friend who walks on by when your mates need you, then you can't expect them to have your back when you're in trouble.

Don't treat relationships like they're transactions. If you enter a friendship thinking to yourself, 'What's in it for me?' I guarantee it won't last.

WHY I HATE GOSSIP

We can make the others around us feel like a million dollars, as if they're unstoppable. The flip side is that we can also do the opposite. The things we say and do have the capacity to crush other human beings in ways we don't always fully appreciate.

Although I communicate as freely as I can about the ideas and issues that interest me (it's no secret that sometimes this goes well, sometimes it doesn't), I'm much warier when it comes to talking about actual human beings.

I don't hate anyone. As much as I can, I try to avoid bad-mouthing other people. Does the world really need to know that I don't like a particular person? Will that improve anybody else's life? What good can come of slagging off somebody I've never met? There have been times when other people have run their mouth off about me in the papers and before I know it, I've had a call from someone in the media asking me what I want to say in response. I tell them what I tell everyone: 'I don't know the guy, I've never met him. I'd been looking forward to meeting the guy, but now I won't.'

I don't want to get drawn into their psychodramas. I don't want to perform for them. And you should look to do the same. Don't bitch, don't gossip, don't backbite. Why waste energy on that sort of negativity? People love the drama so much that they forget what this sort of behaviour leads to. Here's a clue: nothing good.

We have approximately 4,000 weeks on this planet. Ask yourself: is this person worth my energy? Then ask yourself an even more important question: what signal would it send to the world if I spent my life slagging other people off? What sort of person would that make me? And what sorts of people would that kind of behaviour attract and repel?

LESSONS

- Your environment is dictated by the people you surround your-selves with. Positive people create a positive environment. So be careful about who you spend your time with, because it will determine who you are.

- Your circle should be filled with people who inspire you to be the best version of yourself. They should fill you with positive energy. If their company leaves you feeling drained, or under-mined, you should ask yourself whether they're someone worth spending time with.

- Never be afraid to ask for help, or seek out the support and advice that others can provide. Life can be tough, it can be challenging, so why make things harder than they need to be by trying to do everything on your own?

- The single most important choice you will make in life is your partner. No human being will have a greater effect on your journey. Make sure you find someone who shares your values and ambitions.

- I've been to war, I've seen people at their very worst, and yet I'm still always going to give others the benefit of the doubt. It's up to them to prove me wrong. So treat people with respect right up until the moment they show you that they don't deserve it.

- True friendship isn't about blowing smoke up each other's arses. When you've got the right people around you, they'll know when you need support – and when you need to be told that you're heading in the wrong direction.

- Don't gossip. Don't talk shit about others behind their back. Do you need me to explain why?

CHAPTER 3

YOU'RE NOT FOCUSING ON YOU

BENEATH OUR BOOTS the bone-dry stones crunched as we edged ever closer through the tangled scrub that surrounded our target.

Amid the crackle of enemy gunfire, our radios would burst into life with the static-edged voices of the team leaders: minimal, abrupt, nobody talking more than was needed. 'Alpha present,' 'Bravo present,' 'Stand by to move.' There was always something reassuring about their unshakeable calm, whatever the situation. Their voices might get louder so they could be heard and understood over the chaos of a firefight, but that confident, unhurried tone almost never changed: 'Charlie 44, Charlie 55: right, we're going to take the eastern compound, you take the western compound. Let me know when the compound's clear. Go, go, go.'

The moment I hit the deck and began crawling forwards towards an enemy compound, I'd always be able to hear my breath coming in jagged gasps. I tried to cover the ground as fast as I could, my nose and mouth filled with the unmistakeable smell and taste of the desert. This was always the first thing I sensed as I leapt out of the helicopter, the sour cocktail of dust, sand and ancient earth that the rotors churn up from the ground. It's the taste of combat, or more precisely, the taste of the *anticipation* of combat. The moment I clocked it I was straight into the game, all my senses heightened, as if somebody had turbocharged my adrenaline.

This is when our training and experience kicked in. This was what we'd prepared for, this was what we lived for.

WAR IS BRUTAL, cruel and unfair. It always leaves pain and tragedy in its wake. I know that. But in the middle of the slaughter there are always strange spaces full of stillness and beauty. I have been a witness to the uncomfortable and yet exhilarating outer edges of human experience. I know the headspinning excitement of victory, and the bone-gnawing sadness of losing friends and comrades.

It was my privilege as an elite soldier to see and feel all of this. This enlargement of my universe was only possible because I'd focused on myself. I'm only sitting here, writing this book, *because* I've been willing to put myself first, even though I know at times doing so has made the lives of people I care for a bit harder. That might seem like a brutal thing to say, but it's true. When I was out doing hardcore operations, I was putting my needs ahead of my family.

Exactly the same was true of climbing Mount Everest or sailing around the Pacific for *Bounty*. In each of these cases I wasn't just removing myself from my family for extended periods of time, I ran the risk of disappearing from their lives for ever. I know how difficult all of this was for Emilie, and I know how lucky I am to have such a supportive, amazing wife. I'm sure it was difficult at times for my kids too.

And yet I also knew that I *needed* to do these things. Being part of the Special Forces was the culmination of years of hard work and dedication – it made me a better, more fulfilled man. Scaling Mount Everest helped me achieve a long-held dream and offered me an extreme challenge at a time when I was desperately searching for one. They were all events that helped me grow and improve. Without them, I wouldn't be the person I am now. If I'd passed these opportunities up, I know that I'd have spent the rest of my life regretting the fact; and I'm pretty sure that that regret would have turned to resentment. The fact that I didn't is because I knew how important it is to focus on yourself.

ONE OF THE biggest lies out there is the idea that it's selfish to focus on yourself. It's seen as somehow self-indulgent, or at least something you shouldn't even begin to think about until you've dealt with everybody else's problems.

There's just one problem with this perspective: it's utter horseshit.

Do you know why? Because everything starts with you. How are you going to be a positive force for the people around you, or in your workplace, if you haven't got your own shit together? How are you going to care for others if you don't know how to care for yourself? You can't become the best version of yourself – the version of you that your kids and friends and partner need to see – by magic, or by crossing your fingers and hoping. It requires sustained work.

But there are great rewards. The better you feel about yourself and your life, the healthier you're going to be. You'll be less vulnerable to illness, more willing to take exercise and engage fully with the world around you. And the happier, healthier and more connected you are, the better a husband, father, friend and colleague you'll be.

The truth is, it's very hard to build a satisfying life for yourself from the scraps left over by other people. At some point, if you want to become the best version of yourself, you have to acknowledge that, and start focusing on *you*.

FIND OUT WHO YOU ARE

The beautiful thing about every single one of us is that we're all so different. Our emotions, fears and weaknesses are as individual to us as our DNA. That's why I can't just hand you a user's guide to being a human being and let you get on with the business of living. We all have to work out who we are – and how we respond to the world – ourselves.

You don't need to do the extreme things I did. You don't need to kick doors down or climb Mount Everest. You just need to ask yourself some questions, because you can't start working on yourself until you know what you're working with. How well do you know yourself? When it comes down to it, do you know what you're capable of? Are you aware of your strengths? Do you know what your weaknesses are?

These might all seem like incredibly easy questions to answer. How could we not know ourselves? After all, we've spent our whole lives inhabiting the same body and mind. And yet in my experience, it's not quite so simple.

For one thing, we're *not* the same person we've always been. We're all in a constant process of evolution, even if we might not realise it. I'd gone through almost my entire career in the military thinking that my destiny was as a Special Forces operator. It was only when I left that I realised that wasn't who I was meant to be. It took even more time, and a hell of a lot of mistakes and anguish, before I began to even come close to working out who I really was.

Another problem is that many of us put up barriers, or try to pretend we're one sort of person, when actually we're somebody completely different. That's something I've noticed when I compare the two different versions of *SAS Australia*. The civilians are there purely for themselves; there's no ulterior motive. They've got issues they need to work through, or they're looking for redemption of some kind. Their emotions are right on the surface straight away. From day one there are tears, tantrums. You don't really need to work too hard to uncover these people's authentic selves.

It's harder when you're dealing with celebrities, because you know that they all have a public persona that they show to the rest of the world. Our job is to rip that down – which I reckon usually takes about forty-eight hours.

That's why it takes guts for celebrities to come on the course – they know that they're going to be exposed. The longer they stay on, the more stones we turn over, the longer they spend looking into the mirror we hold up to their face. We're there to strip every layer away until we uncover their true self.

What I tell them is: 'I want to see you. I don't want to see the sportsperson or the version of yourself you present to advertisers, I don't even want to see you as a role model. I need to see you as you really are. No crocodile tears. No acting. I can see right through all that. Persist with it and your number will be taken and you'll be gone, off the course.'

The course itself is designed so that people struggle at every stage. We want to see how people deal with failure.

We want to see what they do when their insecurities are revealed. Ultimately, we want the chance to identify their weakness. Once we've done that, we home in on it. This is not or punish or torture them, but to see if they really are who they say they are. The weakness is the chink in the armour we need to begin that process.

A lot of the time, three or four days in, when we show the celebrity exactly who they are, stripped down to their bare bones, and ask them if they like what they see, the answer is no. That's the point when a lot of them VW (voluntarily withdraw). They feel far too vulnerable. It's clear that they *need* that persona. It's what protects them. And, more often than not, they prefer the version of themselves they show the public to the person that they really are.

It's really brave to strip away the edited version of yourself you show the world, but it's also a necessary process. I understand how it's uncomfortable for people when you talk to them about their flaws. They retreat into themselves, put a brick wall around the thing they don't want discussed. They think they're protecting themselves. They're not. They're just blocking 20 or 30 per cent of who they are. You're only going to get to that next level by acknowledging those weaknesses and insecurities.

Because the moment you look in the mirror and can say to yourself, 'Yeah, these are my demons,' is the moment you can begin to work on them. Until you've identified a problem you cannot solve it.

The third problem is that most of us struggle to make the time and space in our lives needed to make that connection with ourselves. There are so many distractions, so many different things tugging at the edges of our attention. But it's so important that I urge you to try to carve out some precious minutes for this crucial process. Shove all of the materialistic stuff aside. Give yourself the breathing space you need to think and reflect. Take the dog for a walk. Before the pandemic I used to go climbing as much as I could. When I had that distance from phones, meetings and family, I could contemplate where I was at in my life, and where I wanted to go next. I could ask myself what about myself I was happy with, and what I felt I needed to improve.

If you need to, treat it like coursework or a project at work. Make a list of your core values. What are the beliefs and behaviours that you cherish? They could be family or honesty, hard work or empathy.

What are your emotional triggers? What are you doing well? What could you do better?

YOU'RE GOING TO be in your own company for twenty-four hours a day for the rest of your life. Nobody else can possibly come close to that. Are you happy with the person you are? If not, your time on the planet is going to be a miserable experience.

Of course, you can't pick your personality off the peg like a new suit. It's something you have to spend time working on and learning about. You will probably have to go out there and learn tough lessons. You might be like the celebrities on *SAS Australia* and find out stuff about yourself that you don't like. But you have to be brutally honest. Lies will just confuse and distort everything. When you lie to yourself you're just setting traps for yourself that one day you're going to blunder into.

Think about the way that you interact with others. Watch closely to see how they respond to your actions and words. Put yourself in their heads. Do you like what you see? It's entirely possible that you might not, in which case you have somewhere to start. You should never be embarrassed that you have flaws, or things that you need to work on. Shame only comes in when you're too complacent either to ask those questions, or to find the solutions the questions demand.

This brutal honesty might seem difficult at the moment, but it's hard work in the short term that will pay off mightily in the long term. Every flaw you remove, every improvement you initiate is another brick taken out of the wall that's standing between you and the best version of yourself.

But always remember that no matter how much effort you put in, you're not going to change overnight. I reckon I'm at 80 per cent of my potential now. On a good day. But that's the result of years of effort and incremental improvement. That callow, shy boy who turned up for his first day of basic training was working at 20 per cent. That's a hell of a journey.

It hasn't always been a smooth progression. I've wasted years trying to figure shit out that I was never going to be able to understand. That's on me. It's a slow process. Sometimes you'll have spells where you're biting huge chunks off. Mostly, though, it's a percentage point here, a percentage point there – what they call marginal gains. And that, by the way, is more than enough.

IT'S OK TO LOOK AFTER NUMBER ONE

You're probably not a selfish person. In fact, you probably have the opposite problem – you're too ready to put others' needs and priorities above your own. A lot of us have unconsciously absorbed the idea that it's our responsibility to make everybody around us happy. We might also think that it's incredibly self-indulgent to take the time to ensure that we're OK, or to do the work needed to keep progressing through life. We've all been indoctrinated to think of spending time working on ourselves as selfish. And I sometimes think that society wants us to be happy enough with crumbs swept from the table. It wants us to squeeze and limit our desires.

Now, I'm not saying you should start behaving like a selfish prick – it's not a zero-sum game! – but what I am saying is that you should be as kind to yourself as you are to others.

Just the act of putting yourself first (even for a little while) can have a psychological impact. Because what you're telling yourself – and everybody else in the world – is that you think that you deserve that effort. It's a statement about your value. And the more you do it, the more your confidence will grow.

It could be really simple things like taking a bit of time for yourself when things get hectic, or treating yourself to clothes that make you feel good. But there are other, more radical things you could consider.

Instead of automatically saying yes to doing things that you don't really want to do, consider trying to say no. Other human beings shouldn't take your kindness and generosity for granted. We learn by imitation. If you're always putting yourself last, then the people around you will do the same. Don't confuse being willing to help with being a pushover. Remember, if you give and give and give without ever thinking of yourself, at some point you'll find yourself trying to run on empty.

Don't be afraid to assert yourself when something you really want to do comes up, even if it clashes with other people's priorities and needs. If those people really love you, if they genuinely have your best interests at heart, then they'll understand. You've been willing to make yourself uncomfortable at times to allow them the time and space they need to become the best version of themselves, so why do you find it so hard to believe that they wouldn't do the same for you?

Emilie is good at this. There will be times when I'm busy planning a trip and she'll ask, 'Do you have to be away for as long as that?' That's not because she's jealous or bitter, but because she's making sure that her needs are being met. A relationship in which one person takes all the time while the other person gives isn't healthy for either party. You might think that turning yourself into some kind of butler who represses himself and his desires so that he can help others is a noble and generous thing to do. It really fucking isn't. It's not good for you, and it's not good for anybody in your vicinity.

Remember that nobody can make you happier. Nobody can make you stronger. Nobody can make you more fulfilled. The only person who can achieve any of this is you. So if you want to make progress towards becoming the best version of yourself – for your benefit as well as for the benefit of those around you – then you're going to have to focus on yourself.

The flip side is that you alone cannot make other people happier, stronger or more fulfilled – and nor is it your responsibility. Support them, help them, be the kind of ally to them you'd want them to be to you, but you cannot take on other people's burdens. You cannot make their happiness your project.

At the same time, it's undeniable that a fulfilled, happy, secure person is always going to be a better friend or partner than someone who has made a habit of suppressing their own desires and needs. As I've said so many times before, we all radiate energy. Every single second of the day. And if you're bored, or angry, or bitter, that's going to fill every room you walk into.

That's why, when I get asked whether I wish I could be at home more, I have two answers. The first is, of course, yes. But I know that's not the reality of life. The more honest answer – given that my career and other commitments mean I have to be working abroad or elsewhere in the country a great deal – is that it's far better that I'm away for 50 to 60 per cent of the year, but that when I'm back I give my family and those I care about the absolute best version of who I am.

The other option is giving my family 95 per cent of my time, but only 50 to 60 per cent of a diminished me. What do my kids gain from spending time with a distracted, anxious, frustrated dad?

DON'T MIX YOUR PRIORITIES AND YOUR RESPONSIBILITIES

Time devoted to yourself should be time dedicated to developing who you are as a human being. Ask yourself, are you progressing in your relationships, with your family, in your professional life? If you're flat-lining, then you've probably given up and it's time for a drastic change.

None of this is a licence to abandon your responsibilities. Prioritising yourself doesn't mean that you can down tools when it comes to your family or your job. You've still got bills to pay! You can't afford to let yourself become someone who – and this really gripes me – talks about babysitting their own kids. What do you mean? That comes with the territory! You're not doing your family a fucking favour by clearing the lowest possible bar of your parental responsibilities.

Before you commit to anything, you must have a clear idea of what your responsibilities are. You need that balance. And that might mean postponing a plan or ambition. That's fine, as long as postponement doesn't really mean cancellation. You can't suppress who you are or try to stop yourself growing.

But there's a difference between self-indulgence and self-improvement. I didn't climb Mount Everest because I wanted time away from my family in an interesting location.

EXERCISE
BE BETTER TO YOU

Concentrating on yourself isn't just about self-improvement. It's also about taking positive steps to make your life better.

When you're connected with yourself, you'll know what makes you happy, and what leaves you sad. Good! Make a concerted effort to ensure that your life is as full of as many of the activities that make you happy as you're able.

List five things you can do each day to help improve the quality of your life. This might be finding five minutes for yourself, or treating yourself to a biscuit, or going for a jog.

I climbed it because I knew that the experience would help me change and grow. I didn't come back the same miserable bastard I'd been before. I came back a better person.

You shouldn't be trying to escape your life, you should be trying to live it. If you climb that mountain to get away from your problems then, guess what, they're still going to be there when you get back. You're just delaying the inevitable moment when you'll have to face them. By contrast, if you're climbing it because you know that the experience will transform you into somebody who's better able to confront the issues lying in wait for you at home, then you're engaged in a deeply positive, life-affirming activity.

Bettering yourself is a prelude to bettering your situation and the people around you. It's not prioritising yourself to go out on the lash in Ibiza for half a week, before spending the other half of the week lying on your living-room sofa.

It's because I put myself first then, that I can support my family now. The investment I made in myself was ultimately an investment in my family's well-being.

LESSONS

- You cannot make any progress in life if you don't focus on yourself. You won't be happy in life if you don't focus on yourself. It's not selfish, it's not self-indulgent. It's absolutely fucking necessary.

- There's only one person on this planet who's responsible for your success and happiness: you. But the opposite is true too: you should never feel as if other people's success and happiness are your burdens to bear.

- Before you focus on yourself, you need to work out who you really are. What are your strengths? What are your weaknesses? What do you need to do to realise your potential? Remember that it's never too late to begin this process of breaking down your emotions and start self-reflecting.

- Your focus on yourself should always be aimed towards a progressive outcome. It's not an excuse to sit on the sofa in your pants. And it should never prevent you from fulfilling your responsibilities.

- If you show the rest of the world that you value yourself, then the rest of the world is far more likely to value you too.

CHAPTER 4

YOU'RE MAKING THE WRONG KINDS OF PLANS

YOU'RE NEVER GOING to get anywhere if you don't know what your destination is. When you don't have goals, your life can too easily become flabby and directionless. Aimlessness might look like freedom but it's really just another kind of prison. Because when you don't know what direction you're going in, you're just as trapped as you would be if you were thrown into a cell.

I have a method for making plans that's individual to me. I believe that you need a What, a Why and a How. But I'm also very sceptical of any plan that commits you rigidly to goals that lie too far into the future. You must give yourself leeway to grab opportunities as they arise.

One good example of the way I set myself targets, and then go about achieving them, would be the clothing line I launched in collaboration with Twinzz, the lifestyle brand run by my close friends Arf and Jez Farooq. Twinzz had done a few clothing items, but the thing they'd enjoyed runaway success with was their caps. They release a new cap and it sells out before you can click your fingers. Our idea was to build a range of activewear – clothes for explorers and adventurers.

This was something that was outside their comfort zone. Although, come to think of it, they weren't quite as far out of their comfort zone as I was. I wonder what the Ant Middleton of 2007 would have said if he'd been told that within fifteen years he'd be designing clothes! Still, we had shared values and a shared enthusiasm for the idea, which in many ways were the most important things. When I do something I want to do it well. No half-measures. No shortcuts. No compromising on anything. The twins had the same mindset. So that was our starting point.

WHAT

If you've got a clear, specific goal then it's easier to visualise the route you need to take to get you there. Vague dreams are just that. Dreams. You must be specific about what it is you want to achieve.

Our only ambition with the clothing line was to launch it into the world with the retail chain Flannels. I was not worried about anything after that. The reason we were so focused on just getting our product into one store was because we wanted a very clearly delineated target.

We could have said, 'Oh we want to be in every shop,' or 'We want to sell X number of items by this date.' Sure, they're great ambitions to have, but are they really achievable?

Of course I wanted it to do well, but that was out of my hands. No matter how hard I work, I can't force customers to get their credit cards out. That's why, although I'd naturally love it if all my books hit number one, I never set that as a target for them. How can you measure your progress if your yardstick for success or failure isn't something you can control?

It was important too that we focused on what we needed to do to get into Flannels specifically. We knew what their criteria were, which gave us something clear to aim for. This wouldn't have been the case if we'd tried to produce clothes that appealed to both Flannels and retailers operating at the other end of the market. We'd have ended up with an awkward compromise product that wouldn't have pleased anyone. As the saying goes, when you try to design a horse by committee you end up with a camel.

So, everything we did was aimed towards achieving that single deal. It kept us all on track, and meant we didn't waste time and energy going down too many blind alleys.

WHY

I also think that when you're thinking about what your aims are, you must be clear about why you're committing yourself to them. As my mate the boxer Tony Bellew says, 'There's no point in climbing into the ring and taking punches if you don't know why you're doing it.'

What is it that you hope to gain? I always want stuff to serve a progressive purpose. When I look at a new project, I need to know that it'll take me that bit closer to becoming the best version of myself. Perhaps you're looking to secure a new job. Great. But why? Is it because you feel as if you're getting stale in your current position and want a new challenge? Or perhaps it's just that you're looking for a higher salary because you're about to become a parent and want to be able to move to a bigger house?

If you're not passionate about the target you want to achieve or can't see what purpose it will serve in your life, then you're going to find yourself in trouble further down the line. Elsewhere in this book I talk about the importance of hard work and commitment. But there's a crucial caveat. Hard work without talent or passion is just hard work. There are millions of people who work hard. They're grafting their balls off, but they're doing something they're not that good at and have next to no enthusiasm for. If you don't care about what you do, you're never going to put your heart and soul into it. It's just drudgery, and what kind of a life is that? A slog with no passion or progression.

If you can't throw yourself wholeheartedly into a particular task or course of action, then what are you doing? Maybe this thing wasn't meant for you. If you're not dedicated to being a father, don't have children. If you're not dedicated to being a teacher, then stay the fuck away from the classroom.

Because when you're not giving everything you'll just bimble along, never really getting anyway, rarely if ever feeling fulfilled, and then one day you'll come to with a jolt and realise your target is as far away as when you started out.

ONCE YOU'VE IDENTIFIED what your motivation is, make sure you hold it close to you. That's the thing that will keep you going when things get wobbly – which, or course, they inevitably will. When you're stressed, when it looks as if everything is stacked against you, it's so important to be able to remind yourself that you're putting yourself through all this shit for a reason.

That's why it really gripes me when I hear about people being told that an important part of the goal-setting is writing them down. If you need to consult a bit of paper because you've forgotten what it was you wanted to achieve, then it's not a goal, it's a daydream. It's in the same territory as the notes kids write to Santa. You should be obsessed with your goals. They should feel tangible, achievable, and they should be something that *you* want, not what you think is expected of you or that you're doing to please somebody else. I want something that I can *taste*.

The clothing line was something that would take me way out of my comfort zone. I knew that by throwing myself into a world that was so alien to me I'd give myself the chance to learn a massive amount. It would expose me to unfamiliar places and people, and I'd pick up new skills. There was also the opportunity it offered to do something meaningful with two guys who are really important in my life. The reason I got into business with them was because of who they *are*. We came up with the vision together, and we believed in it together. I was really attracted to the collaborative nature of the project and the idea that at the end of it we'd have created something really tangible we could all be proud of.

All of that meant that it was something I knew I was willing to take punches for.

HOW

You're never going to know every detail of every stage of the process in advance. And that's OK. It's important to retain that nimble mindset – you can't afford to be in the position where you start panicking because something has

turned out differently from the way you imagine
ing.

But you do need to have a good idea of what you've g
to do if you're going to achieve your targets. What resources
will you require? Do you need to ask anyone in particular
for help or advice? Can you think of any problems that
might crop up along the way? If so, can you prepare potential solutions?

For us, one of the most important priorities was identify-
ing who was going to take on what responsibilities. We all
knew we had something to offer, and were all humble
enough to know that so did each of the other players. It
would have derailed everything if I'd pretended I had expertise in areas which, if I was going to be honest, I was barely
aware of. We were all as keen to learn as to teach.

The Twinzz knew what technology to use – the sort of
machinery involved in manufacturing clothes that were
resistant to wear and tear. They also already had established
relationships with factories and their logistics game was
bang on. So, of course, that interested me. I had my own
experience of operating in hostile environments, discovering
what sorts of clothing work in what sorts of situations. I
knew what I was comfortable wearing, whether that was
climbing mountains, trekking, running, jumping out of helicopters. I knew what I wanted and what would work for me.

Flannels injected their own expertise and know-how into
the process. Their commitment to quality is unparalleled

and matched our own. Their threshold for what they'll stock is really impressive. They're never going to sell any old tat off the street.

We cycled through parts of China, Taiwan and Portugal looking for the right place to make the clothes. A lot of the top brands already operate in Portugal, and the ability to be able to visit the factories on a reasonably regular basis was also attractive. In our first meeting they told us that they only produced high-end clothes, almost as if they thought that would put us off. But, of course, that's exactly what we wanted to hear. At that point we flew out so that we could meet them face-to-face.

There were nine separate prototypes between showing them our first sketch-out draft and getting the finished product. I loved that, loved the whole process. Whenever I had spare time I'd try to drive up to Manchester or fly to Portugal. For a while, things like holidays and a social life had to take second place.

THE DAY THAT the launch day came around I was ecstatic. It was such a privilege to see clothes instore that I'd help design. And it was so exciting watching people buying them and being as excited about them as I was. Honest to God, I didn't care if it succeeded or not. I was just so proud we'd achieved what we'd set out to do. In the course of two years we'd gone from talking about the clothes to making them.

We'd started out with an idea, and now I held a physical manifestation of that idea in my hands.

NEVER FORGET

What I tried to keep front and centre of my mind throughout the whole project was the thought that we might fail. Not because I was afraid of failure, but because I knew that the outcome wasn't the most important element of the enterprise. I didn't want to be so focused on 'success' that I blinded myself to all the amazing experiences I was gaining at every stage of the project. If at the end of the process Flannels decided not to stock the clothes, I didn't want to feel that everything we'd done had been wasted.

DON'T LOOK TOO FAR AHEAD

Where I differ from so many other people is that although I set and follow short-term goals, I generally steer away from medium- and long-term goals. And contrary to a lot of the received wisdom about targets, I don't like to commit to a rigid timescale.

That's because I believe that when you get too set on one target, and too attached to a particular schedule, you forget how exciting and full of possibility the rest of the world is.

This means you risk developing a dangerous kind of tunnel vision. That tunnel vision is exactly what elite athletes or tech visionaries need, but the conditions of their lives are completely different to mine, and I'd be willing to bet are pretty different to yours too. A too-close focus on long-term goals actually ends up being a distraction because it stops you seeing what's really there in front of you. An opportunity might come along and you're so fixated on a particular vision of your future that you let it pass you by.

Out of ten chances that present themselves to me, I might only be pulled towards three. And only one of those three will come to anything. But it's important to me that at the very least I'm open to them all. What if one of those opportunities is life-changing?

Who Dares Wins changed almost every aspect of my existence. But when I got the call from a producer asking if I was interested in coming in for an audition, I was trying to build a security business in Africa. The idea of going on television or becoming an author didn't figure in my plans. It wasn't that I thought they were impossible goals; they were literally inconceivable.

I scrapped a business that was already lucrative, and promised to be even more so further down the line, in order to take a risk. On balance I reckoned I'd maybe get one shot at one series, but I also had a feeling that there was something there. If I got it right, if I was allowed to run the show the way that I wanted it to be run, we could end up making something special. I asked myself whether I was likely to get another chance like this. Probably not, was the honest answer. So I went for it. As it turned out, the show was a big hit, and it's been the springboard for so many other amazing things. But I'm still trying not to look more than two years ahead. I just want to keep focused on what's in front of me right now.

Always make sure that you keep your eyes open. Stay alert. Don't let an exciting opportunity that's right under your nose slip away because you're staring miles ahead at a distant target that you might never even reach.

ONE LAST THING

If you want to achieve your ambitions, whatever they are, you must be ready to put a shift in. It doesn't matter if you've devised the best plan in the world. It doesn't matter if you've colour-coded all of your schedules. Unless you're willing to graft and graft, your goals will go unrealised. You have to be willing to keep going when everybody else has given up. You have to be willing to sacrifice holidays, weekends, evenings. Most of my greatest achievements have been earned where nobody else can see. So, if you want to make your dreams become a reality, you're going to have to roll up your sleeves.

LESSONS

- If you don't make any plans or set yourself targets, you'll lead an aimless, unsatisfying existence. You'll struggle to ever make the sort of progress you need.

- Be as clear as you can be about what you want to achieve. The more specific you are, the easier it will be to construct a path to success.

- You must have a why as well as a what. That's what will keep you going when times get tough.

- Don't chain yourself to rigid long-term plans. You should always remain alert to the new opportunities that life will throw up. Don't be afraid of making abrupt shifts in direction or focus. Prioritise your instincts over schedules and tick lists.

- A plan is only ever as good as the work you're willing to invest in it. If you're not ready to graft, you're never going to reach your goals.

CHAPTER 5

YOU'RE A FOLLOWER, NOT A LEADER

ONE THING I hear a lot from people is that they go through their days feeling cut adrift. They can't seem to grab hold of the reins of their life or exert their will. Somehow, they always end up doing what somebody else wants them to do, not what they themselves want to do. Perhaps they just want to fit in and please others; or it might be that they're not confident enough about their own judgement, so they always end up deferring to the men and women around them.

But the net result is always the same. In my experience, people who let others make their decisions for them are more stressed and unhappy than those who are in charge of their own destiny. They feel powerless and struggle to motivate themselves. It's difficult for those who are followers rather than leaders in their own life to know what to do, and their growth is stunted as a result.

I'm not afraid of the world because I rule my own life. But I also understand how hard it is to resist the pressure to follow a path that goes against your instincts, especially in those confusing scenarios where, although you're pretty sure what you *don't* want to do, it's less clear to you what you *do* want to do. There are so many who want to push you in a particular direction: partners, schools, companies. And, of course, there's always the expectation to conform to what society deems 'correct'.

I remember one occasion early on in my military career when someone tried to push me in a direction that felt completely wrong to me. On that day I'd gone in to see a warrant officer, a guy I'd always respected and liked, to talk about taking a PTI's course – I wanted to get the qualification to become a physical training instructor.

As I entered, I noticed that he was holding a letter. This caught me off-guard. *What the hell is this about?* It was only when he showed it to me that it made sense. Not long beforehand I'd been asked to translate for a French colonel who was visiting. We had three great days working side by side and it seems that I'd impressed everyone with the job I'd done. Soon afterwards, my unit received a letter full of praise for me. Once I'd read the letter, the warrant officer congratulated me on how well I'd represented the squadron. So far, so good, I thought He was brimming over with enthusiasm. 'Absolutely brilliant.' Then the mood shifted a little bit.

'Why not go down that route?' the warrant officer asked. 'Why don't you train as an interpreter? Your French is an amazing skill to have. You're fluent and I don't understand why you haven't tried to take advantage of it before now. There's so much you can do with it.'

I didn't know what to say. Whatever else I thought about the army, I knew that I loved hardcore soldiering. When I joined it was because I thought I wanted to see more of the world. It felt like a ticket away from the beautiful but far too sedate village in Normandy that I'd come to call home. And although I hadn't travelled quite as much as I thought I would, that didn't matter because I'd fallen in love with the craft of soldiering. Being a warrior was no longer a means to an end to me – it *was* the end. I was fascinated by it all. I wanted to be a sniper and then perhaps join the Special Forces. I knew I wasn't ready right now, but I thought these were things I could work towards.

'I'm delighted that they were pleased with the job I did, sir,' I told him, 'and I'm really grateful that you're thinking about my career like this. But that's not what I want to do.'

'You're not built for soldiering.' All the cheer had left his voice.

'Sir, with all due respect, I don't agree.' I was trying to stay calm, even though every atom in my body suddenly seemed to be screaming at me. I'd worked so hard to get to this point and he was casually suggesting that I just throw everything into the bin. Fuck. Him.

'Look, Middleton, I'm trying to do you a favour here. I'm not going to insult you by hiding behind pretty words. You're too small. That's a fact. You've done well to get this far, but ultimately your physique's going to be a liability. It's a real shame. But there it is. There's a six-month translator's course in Beaconsfield. You'd come out with a qualification. And, between you and me, it'd be a nice, easy spell. Think about it. No need to rush your decision.'

He must have thought that this would be the clinching argument. In a sense, it was. It removed any doubt I felt about the course I wanted my career to take. I didn't want an easy life. I wanted to be challenged, I wanted stuff to be a bit uncomfortable. Six months of pissing about pretending to be a student just wasn't me. It was exactly what I'd joined the army to avoid. And the thing is, I didn't need a bit of paper to tell me I could speak French. At the time, I spoke it as well as I did English.

The WO dismissed me with a patronising wave of the hand. I'm fairly certain that once I'd left the room, he forgot our conversation almost immediately. He'd told me what he thought was best for me, and had no reason to trouble himself any further about my future. But my head was buzzing with it.

Back in our barracks I told a mate about what had just happened.

'Beaconsfield!' he exclaimed, his eyes lighting up in excitement. 'That's where they send all the officers, isn't it? It'll be a six-month jolly.' He was almost rubbing his hands with glee. 'You'll be mixing with the ruperts, treated like you're a member of the fucking royal family.'

'I don't want a six-month jolly. I want to be a soldier.'

He looked at me, stupefied. It was as if I'd told him I was planning to travel to the moon. I began to question myself. The WO's words nagged away at me. I could see where he was coming from. It's hard not to develop a bit of a complex when someone says something as categorical as that. Doubts began to creep in through the crack that his comments had opened up in my self-belief. Maybe he's right? Maybe I am too small? No matter how hard I trained, I was never going to be able to alter some fundamental things about myself. There was no amount of time spent in the gym that was going to transform me into a 6 ft 6 Viking. And I had struggled in the past. But the point was, although I'd struggled, I'd made it through. I was still only nineteen, still growing, and with the drive and desire I had I knew I'd only grow stronger.

More than that, the journey he was proposing for me went against everything I wanted. It went against everything I knew about myself. I could have gone with the flow. It would have been so much easier to do that. But I knew I'd never be happy or content if I allowed someone else to make my decisions for me.

I was being pulled in a different direction. I knew that I owed it to myself to follow that energy to see where it led me.

For a few days afterwards I could feel my thoughts shifting and reforming. To begin with, I couldn't quite work out what I needed to do. Then everything crystallised: I realised it was time for a change. The route that the WO wanted me to take wasn't right for me. Nor, in fact, was anything about the environment in the Paras – it was becoming increasingly clear that my face just didn't fit. There was still nothing I wanted more than to become an elite soldier, but paradoxically at this moment in my life, the army wasn't the place for me. A few weeks later, I started the process of leaving.

SOMETIMES I THINK about what my life would have been like if I'd followed the path that the warrant officer had tried to send me on. Of course, events could have taken me in all sorts of directions. I'm not even going to try to speculate about what I might have ended up doing (although I'm pretty sure I wouldn't have enjoyed the same sorts of highs and lows). But I do have a pretty good idea of how I might have ended up feeling. Trapped. Bitter. Resentful.

That's what happens when you go against all of your instincts and let other human beings govern your life.

I'd have become a decision-taker, not a decision-maker.

When you make a decision, you own it. For better or worse, you own its consequences. But the point is that you're still the author of your fate. You're acting in accordance with your will. When you let somebody else take those calls on your behalf, you're letting somebody else write your story. You'll for ever be responding to their agenda, their priorities. That always leads to bitterness, frustration and resentment. Because you know, your body knows, that you should be doing more. Why would you ever want to be in the position of watching somebody else thrive because they took decisions you didn't have the courage or the will to make yourself? 'I could have done that.' 'Well, you didn't, so move on.' Shoulda, woulda, coulda.

You need to take yourself to those places, because nobody else is going to take you. I'm not naïve. I know that it's harder to be somebody who forces the pace, who makes decisions. But when you're always just going along for the ride, then somebody else will always be driving. It might be fun and interesting. And yet you're not at the wheel.

ONLY YOU

The surest way to end up trapped behind the wall is to live your life as a follower, not a leader. So don't be passive. Don't sit there waiting for somebody else to tell you what to do or think.

The first thing you need to accept is that you're the person who has ultimate responsibility for how your life works out. You can't rely on others to save you. You can't rely on them to always have your best interests in mind, or even to know what you want and need from your life. That has to come from you.

BE THE LEADER OF YOUR OWN LIFE

You need to lead yourself. And the great thing is, we're all capable of leading, even if most of the time we don't realise it. We think leaders are officers in the army, or managers at a company, or sports captains. We don't realise that leadership isn't about the badge on your chest or the band on your arm. It's about taking responsibility, being decisive, being dedicated. A good leader knows who we are, and what our strengths and weaknesses are. They also want us to improve. Why not apply exactly the same principle to your own day-to-day life?

The ultimate leadership is to be the leader of your own existence. What I mean by that is that you have to approach your own life with a leader's mindset. Imagine that you're a leader who has been given the task of maximising your own personal development. Everything you do has to help achieve this objective. That means prioritising your own needs and ambitions. That means demanding as much as you can from yourself. That's the mindset you should have when it comes to your own development.

It's almost like a psychological trick, but I find it really helps you enter the right headspace. And if that's the mentality you adopt in your life, then there's very little that can stop you.

TRUST YOUR INSTINCTS

Other human beings will try to shape your life for you. They might be parents, teachers, friends or colleagues. A lot of the time they'll be like that warrant officer who tried to make me take the translator's course. They'll give you a whole list of convincing reasons why you should follow the route they've suggested, and you won't necessarily have a decent response. All you'll have is a feeling that it's not right for you.

In these situations it's very easy to let yourself be swayed. You tell yourself that they probably know better and that they have your best interests at heart. So you pretend you haven't felt that niggling discomfort. You just hope that those doubts will disappear once you get your feet under the table at the new job your boss wanted you to apply for, or once you really get to grips with the subject that your parents 'suggested' you study at university.

But this rarely happens. We know ourselves better than anybody else. Although we should generally listen to advice from other people – especially those who have more experience and expertise than we do – we should also make sure that it's us and us alone who are making decisions about our future. That often means paying proper attention to the sometimes quite unclear messages our body sends us.

If something doesn't *feel* right, then it's worth asking yourself very serious questions as to whether you should be doing it. Doing something because you know it will please other people isn't a good-enough reason to ruin your own happiness or development. And just because somebody else claims they have your best interests at heart doesn't mean that they actually do – only you know what's best for you.

Your instincts are there for a reason, so make sure you listen to them.

I DID IT MY WAY

I've always done things my way. And that can get people hot and bothered. It happened on *Mutiny*: 'That's not how sailors do this!' No, but it's how *I* do it.

I realise that social media is driving that desire to compare ourselves with others. Even though we all know deep down that all we're seeing is a highlights reel, it's still hard to resist. That's something innate in us. When we look admiringly at other people's strengths, we tend to forget about or underrate the qualities that we possess. We're in such a rush to praise that person that we overlook the fact that they have weaknesses too.

You're never going to be a peace with yourself if you're trying to compare yourself with others, or imitate them. You're not them and you never will be. If there's something about them that inspires you, then great, grab it. But you need to absorb that quality into who you are, not wear it on the surface like a badly fitting borrowed suit.

When you try to ape someone else, you're diminishing who you are. You're cutting yourself off from your own unique potential. You're strangling your ability to grow.

Instead of focusing on becoming somebody else, focus on you. You'll learn so much more, gain so many more rewards by making the most of the resources that are already within you.

When you're younger, you'll probably audition lots of different versions of who you are. In your youth you're much more magpie-like, taking traits from a whole range of people, often without thinking about it too much. You adopt the mannerisms of other people, copy their clothes. Sometimes you might imitate the way they dress. That's natural. One way of discovering who you are is by working out who you're not. What would be worrying is if you're still doing this later in life.

There has to come a moment when you realise: 'Shit, I've got to do me.' Because if you're not doing that when you enter the big wide world, then very soon you're going to find yourself completely lost.

LESSONS

- If you live your life as a follower, not a leader, then you'll for ever be living life on somebody else's terms. Be a decision-maker, not a decision-taker.

- Be a leader in your own life. Look out for your interests. Take responsibility. Demand the highest standards and the greatest levels of commitment. Do everything a good leader would for their team ... but do it for yourself.

- People will try to influence you to do things that they say are in your best interests. But if you take a step down that path and it doesn't *feel* right to you, then that's a sign that it probably *isn't* right for you. Don't be afraid to follow your instincts.

- Perhaps you're not yet the person you want to be, but then who is? We're all works in progress. But what you cannot do is pretend to be somebody you're not. You'll never get anywhere worth going by imitating other people. Stay true to yourself.

CHAPTER 6

YOU FOCUS ON SYMPTOMS, NOT CAUSES

PEOPLE THINK THAT they're creatures of comfort. They convince themselves that what they want is to feel safe and take the easy option. They're 9 to 5 people who tell themselves that they're happy spending eight hours a day in the same office with the same people, then coming home to eat the same meal before watching the same show on TV. They wake up the next morning, and the whole process begins again. It's a good life. It's what society tells them is the 'right' life. They're doing everything that's been asked of them. They're meeting other people's expectations. And there are many who genuinely need that sort of grinding routine, who actually thrive on it.

I'm the complete opposite of that. I want complete, unanswerable freedom. I want to do what I want to do, when I want to do it, how I want to do it. I want to be a slave to nobody and nothing. I don't want to feel like I need to apologise to anyone for anything. I'm not there yet, but that's what I'm working towards.

When I get too comfortable, I feel myself falling away. I'm not a normal person – I follow my standards. I'm wired differently. I'm sporadic. I don't fit into that 9 to 5 world because I'm so energetic and active. Here's the thing: I don't think that I'm alone in being like this. I believe that the world is full of people who have the same instincts and energy as me. But the difference is that they feel compelled to follow other people's expectations. Along the way, their own ambitions and aspirations get squashed.

It starts early. I was lucky that when I was a boy I could let all my energy out. But I don't know how many kids these days have the same chance. Things are so controlled and restrictive. They certainly don't have the freedom I had. They're being pushed into tests and exams from the age of four. They're told who and what they are, and what box they need to fit themselves into. And the moment they're not in the box, the moment they're not accountable to society, people get very uneasy.

That's why people seek solace in what I call synthetic highs. They're not living the life they want, but at the same time they see no way they can start to lead a different existence. They settle for a decent job with a decent house and stop asking for any better. Along the way they suppress their capabilities and their need for more. They're in a cage. Maybe they fight against it for a bit, and yet after a while they forget that the bars are even there.

Drinking, partying, drugs, one-night stands all offer them a release. It's wild behaviour that's by and large tolerated by society because ultimately it helps keep people in their place.

They chase these synthetic highs because they don't believe they can get them naturally from their day-to-day existence.

I used to get my highs through drinking and fighting because everything else in my life seemed to lack meaning. That was true even when I was in the Special Forces – when I'd reached the absolute pinnacle of my trade, when I was doing the most exhilarating, significant job there is.

If I wasn't training or fighting, I'd go fucking rogue. Between tours there would always be a bit of downtime. Some of the lads would go out surfing or climbing, while me and a couple of others went on the piss all the time. Bar. Club. Bar. Club. Go again. That was my headspace at the time, even though I was getting natural highs from the combat simulation. At the time I couldn't differentiate between the two. A high was a high. But it was only when I left that the drinking and fighting spiralled out of control.

I needed the adrenaline those things gave me; the buzz of getting into a scrap and having no idea whether I'd come out on top. I remember that I used to say to people, 'Oh, I'm due a good row.'

Now I'd never go after a problem, but when it came you'd better believe I embraced it. Whatever the rest of the world might think about me, I'm not a violent person. And the thing I hated most about this life I was leading was the aftermath of the fights I got into. 'Fuck, I've broken that guy's jaw.' 'Fuck, look at his face.' I'd find myself disturbed by the horror of what I was capable of, which was ultimately the horror of who I was. I was never bothered by the prospect of being in trouble with the police. I could take a charge or a night in the cells without blinking. What I found hard to live with was the knowledge of the damage I'd caused. Still, I was trapped in a cycle that saw me make the same mistakes over and again.

We need that rush of adrenaline because it's our natural instinct to be like that. If you capture a lion and then raise its cubs in captivity, feeding them by hand, surrounding them with human beings, why do you still keep those cubs in a cage? Because lions know nothing else but their instincts. You're guarding against that one time. That one single time. Because their inner nature is always there.

Human beings are the same. Every single one of us. We all have a beast inside us and we all need a release valve. Our natural instinct is to deal with stuff in the easiest way possible. We feel depressed, so we go out and drink rather than try to tackle the cause of that depression. It's easier to go to the pub and get wrecked than it is to face up to your deep-seated problems.

SYNTHETIC HIGHS, HOWEVER, can only ever act as a sticking plaster. They can make you feel better for a few hours, maybe a whole night, but once they wear off you'll find yourself hungover, or with a bruise over your eye and a belly full of regrets.

A synthetic high is never going to be progressive. It saps your time, money and energy and leaves you with nothing. It's much better to find other, less destructive ways of venting that pent-up frustration.

There are still times when I get a surge of the feeling that once upon a time made me think to myself, 'Oh, I'm due a good row.' But now, instead of putting myself in the sort of situation that might lead to a vicious tear-up in a nightclub carpark, I go out on a track and push my car as fast as I can. I come home and almost the first thing that Emilie notices is the way that my hands are shaking from the adrenaline that's still coursing through my veins.

I also go climbing or mountaineering. What excites me about this are the questions you have to ask yourself over and over again: 'What if I fall here?' 'What if I take the wrong step?' I love the frightening thrill that comes with looking at your equipment and asking yourself: 'Is this enough?' I live off that buzz. There's nothing more exciting that being on a rockface. Your life is in your hands.

These might not be practical responses for you. It's possible that they might be the last thing you'd ever consider doing. But that doesn't mean you can't find your own equivalent. Look for something that forces your body and mind out of their normal sedate rhythms. I know that exercise – it could be a weekly game of five-a-side or just a run you grab during your lunchbreak – works for lots of people. It can be a really effective way of expelling the rage and resentment that tends to build up in all of us.

THE LEAKING BOAT

There is of course a further step you can take. Whether you're chasing synthetic highs or have progressed to their more natural equivalents, you're still basically just treating the symptoms of the problem, not its causes. You're giving that lion cub a toy to play with, or a slightly bigger space in which to pace up and down. What you're not doing is setting it free so that it can live the life that every single strand of its DNA demands that it should. For years and years after my father's death, I was blindly trying to deal with the symptoms I was experiencing, but never gave a thought to addressing their cause. I felt grief and anger, and these emotions governed so much of my behaviour. That's why I spent so much time getting drunk out of my skull, or scrapping with idiots.

It was only once I started really grappling with my demons that I began to really make progress as a man. I realised that I'd been like someone adrift on the ocean in a boat with a massive hole in it. But rather than fixing that hole, I'd been using a shitty little tin can to try to bail out all the water that was flooding in. Although I was – just about – managing to keep that little boat from sinking into the depths, it was exhausting, unpleasant work, and became ever harder the older I got. It was only a matter of time before I went under.

I realise that this is delicate, complex territory. Not everybody will recognise their own story in my specific circumstances. Losing my father had a unique effect on me, so even if you've experienced the same trauma, you might have responded to it in a completely different way. But if you're getting fucked-up every weekend, if you can't hold down a relationship, if you have days when you find yourself engulfed by rage at everyone and everything, isn't it worth looking at your life to see whether there are underlying reasons that dictate the sorts of choices you make? Is it because you're bored witless by your job? Is it because you feel suffocated by other people's expectations? Are you struggling in secret with your mental health?

Don't you owe it to yourself, and to those who care for you and rely upon you, to find out? Ask yourself: why are *you* feeling like this? Why do *you* keep doing the same things? Why do *you* keep making the same mistake? Do *you* know yourself well enough to recognise what's happening and why?

The longer you hold off from asking those questions, the longer you're going to stay lost in the void.

Because when your focus is on dealing with symptoms rather than causes, you're only going to end up suppressing yourself. You're placing self-imposed limits on your potential. It's like deliberately playing life on the hardest mode possible.

SOME OF THE people facing the biggest challenges are ex-military. As I've previously mentioned, readjusting to the messy realities of civvy street after years in the rigid, ordered army can be difficult. Many of them now feel no sense of belonging, as they no longer have a sense of purpose and achievement.

I remember one guy, Mikey, who messaged me a few times. He told me that he'd read all of my books and they'd really helped him at some of his lowest moments. But he was getting up to a lot of stupid stuff. He'd tell me things and I'd think, 'Fuck me, you're sailing pretty close to the wind.' When I didn't hear from him for a while I assumed he'd got back on the straight and narrow, and everything had settled down for him. The last thing I'd said was to keep going back to the books. 'Don't think that you're ever done. The work never stops. And if my books have worked for you, then I'm so pleased and honoured.'

Then maybe a year after we'd last been in contact I got a text message from his girlfriend. She told me that he'd been given a life sentence after getting embroiled in a violent altercation. It was a story I'd heard so many times before, but one that never fails to affect me deeply.

'He's asking how he can get through everything,' she said

when we spoke on the phone a bit later the same day. 'What can he do?'

'Tell him that I told you to say this,' I replied.

'Tell him, "You need to hold yourself accountable, you've got to take it on the chin. If you're guilty of the crime you've been sent down for, then you've got to face up to it. Learn from it. Do what you can to make amends. You're not the first person to make a bad mistake. You won't be the last. You're at your lowest point now. Acknowledge that you're going to be in there for ten years. That it's out of your hands now, there's nothing you can do.

'"But do you know what *is* in your hands? How you spend those ten years. Don't let it become dead time. Make every day count. You say you've read all my books. And yet you're here. It's like you needed this for them to actually make sense. Because if you'd been actioning it, you wouldn't be looking at a life sentence.

'"Your life has been stripped back to its most simple elements. You don't have to deal with many of the complicated responsibilities that are an inescapable part of life outside your prison's four walls. You know what time you have to get up, what time you'll eat, what time you can leave your cell. There's always going to be a roof over your head and food on the table. There's almost nothing you can do to exert any influence on what happens on the outside. If some road-rage prick starts shouting at your girlfriend, what are you going to do?

'"So, you could walk out on your exit date having done nothing except watch the clock, or you could have improved yourself. It's not just that you have lots of time to self-reflect, time to really get to know yourself. There are so many opportunities to gain qualifications.

'"Take each day as it comes. Do something new and positive every twenty-four hours. It might be reading a book. It might be signing up for a course. It might be doing something that helps you move up through the prison hierarchy. Use *everything* you can.

'"Don't fall into the trap of planning a life that begins on the day that you're released. Don't pretend that what's happening here and now isn't your real life. Don't pretend that your real existence is waiting ahead of you once this or that has happened. THIS. RIGHT. NOW. This is your real life.

'"You should be doing so much that your outlook as it was is completely different to your outlook now. You need to have ambitions and expectations that dwarf whatever you currently want from life.

'"You will never have a better chance to focus on yourself."'

We still touch base every now and then. I sent him signed copies of my books. We talk about them. We talk about the problems we both face, and the progress we have and haven't been able to make.

SEIZE THE DAY

The thing about Mikey is that prison is going to give him a chance to address the things that he's struggled with for so long. You don't do the stuff he did if you're not carrying some serious issues around with you on your shoulders. But he has the opportunity to make sure that by the time he gets out he's a different person, with stronger foundations.

You don't need to wait to reach your lowest point before you do the same. If you're struggling with your mental health, now is the time to open up and talk to somebody, whether it's a close friend or a therapist. If you're so unchallenged by the job you're in that the only way you can rid yourself of all your excess energy is to cause trouble every Saturday and Sunday, now is the time to think about a change of career. If you're in a relationship that makes you unhappy and leaves you full of self-loathing, now is the time to end it.

You have to live with yourself for every second of the time you have left on this earth. Why not do everything you can to make the most of it?

LESSONS

- So many of us find ourselves living lives suppressed by society's expectations. We seek a release from the pressure and frustration we feel in synthetic highs, like drinking and fighting. Why not swap these empty synthetic highs for more progressive natural ones?

- It wasn't until I faced up to the consequences of my father's death that I really turned my life around. At some point you'll realise that it's better to confront the causes of your problems rather than desperately trying to treat their symptoms. Do what you need to do to address the issues that lie at the heart of your problems.

- Honest conversations are always difficult. But they're also the best sorts of conversation to have, because you're not wasting anybody's time. You're never going to be able to find the solution to a problem if you're not able to be honest about what it is you're facing up to.

CHAPTER 7

YOU GIVE UP
TOO EASILY

NOTHING CAN PREPARE you for the ways in which fame, even in its mildest varieties, can bend the life you had before out of shape. I don't think I was ready for the level of attention I got. Actually, I know I wasn't. Just ask Emilie. I still find it strange that people recognise me in the street. And there isn't a book long enough to describe the complicated, and often uncomfortable, relationship anyone even semi-famous has with the media.

I'm not here to complain. My career on television and as an author has brought me brilliant things. And the thing I never expected, the thing that I feel blessed by, is the fact that I've been given a platform that I can use to help others. I don't want to sound like I'm preaching, but I mean this. It's so important to me. I'm really lucky that from time to time I can make a difference, even in tiny ways, to other people's lives.

That makes those occasions when I'm confronted by a story, or a situation, that I can do nothing about all the harder to bear. There's one guy in particular I'm thinking about. We met while I was signing books in a store near where he was from. I could tell that Jack was a bit of a lost soul even before he'd opened his mouth. The harsh artificial lights of the shopping centre we were in weren't doing any of us any favours, but they were especially harsh on his face. They showed how gaunt and pale he was, how thin his hair had got, and seemed to pick out every single line on his face. He seemed almost afraid to be there.

He wasn't after advice, not really. What he wanted was consolation. Jack grew up in a provincial town, which he told me he'd hated. He never felt as if he really fitted in with any of the other kids at his school and spent most of his time counting down the days until he could escape. For him, that escape was art school. He thought that once he was among like-minded people he could leave the drabness and pettiness of his old life behind for ever.

Even Jack would probably admit that art school was always going to struggle to live up to those expectations. It's unrealistic to see any one thing as a magic ticket. Still, he told me he wasn't prepared for what happened when he arrived there. He discovered that he fucking *hated* it.

He'd gone right through his teenage years thinking that he was creative, the fact that he excelled at art forming a big plank of his identity. It was what set him apart from every-one else in his class. Of course, he didn't magically get worse at drawing or photography when he arrived at art school, he just found himself surrounded by other kids who were all as good as him. And some of them were better. Quite a lot better.

'I couldn't cope with that,' he told me. 'I know it sounds stupid, but it sent my head in a spin. It just sort of upended my sense of who I was and what I could offer the world.'

Jack's confidence took a real knock almost immediately, and never really recovered. Still, he did his best. 'I reckon I was the only one on my course who went to every lecture, every seminar,' he said ruefully. 'And I threw everything I had at my end-of-year project.'

But he only just scraped a pass.

'That hit me so hard. It confirmed all the doubts I'd been haunted by over the last months. I just thought to myself, "I'm not good enough, what am I even doing here?"'

The tipping point came when one of his tutors tried to give him some advice about how he could improve the following year.

'I don't know why I reacted so badly, but I did. Hurt pride I guess. I just told him to fuck off and stormed out. Apart from coming back to my halls during the summer to pick up all my stuff from my room, that was the last time I set foot in that art school. Or any art school. Although I didn't know that at the time.'

Jack went back to live with his parents. He thought it would be a temporary arrangement. Initially he told himself that he would go back to art school, that it wasn't too late to try again. He started doing some casual work in a factory.

Then years went past, almost without him noticing, and one day he realised that it was too late. He wasn't ever going to go back to art school, and, worse, he was stuck in the town that he thought he'd escaped.

'I've gone past the point of having regrets now,' he said. 'I spent ages blaming everyone around me. I was so angry, I couldn't believe that nobody had tried to stop me – although of course they did, I just wasn't listening. So I've made my peace with the stupid fucking decision I made, but I'm still struggling to get used to the consequences.'

QUITTING CAN FEEL like the easiest thing in the world.

But the fact is, that most of the time quitting only offers a temporary release from discomfort. All you're really doing is exchanging a moment's relief for a lifetime's worth of regret. You end up bitter and sad like Jack, because when you look back at your past you realise that you weren't beaten by circumstances, or bad luck, or a stronger opponent; you were beaten by yourself.

You cannot afford to let yourself become one of those people who start out on their journey full of enthusiasm, and then, as soon as there's even a tiny bump in the road, turn around and go back, telling themselves, 'Ah well, it wasn't meant to be.' You can't afford to convince yourself that unless every single door swings wide open for you, there's no point persisting. You can't afford to not realise that, sometimes, it's up to you to break those doors down. You can't afford to be like Jack.

YOU'RE STRONGER THAN YOU THINK

The thing you need to appreciate – in those moments when you're overwhelmed by the temptation to throw in the towel – is that you've survived 100 per cent of your bad days. How amazing is that? You're so much stronger than you believe, so why are you telling me right *now* that your life is fucked? You're still here, you're still standing. You've beaten everything that's ever been thrown at you. So why do you think that now is the moment when that perfect record is going to come to an end? Why *wouldn't* you smash whatever's coming down the road?

You've proved that you've survived, so why not start living? And how do you start living? By building yourself up.

I think it takes us all a while to realise how resilient we are. Sometimes we need to take a step back and appreciate how much we've survived, and how much stronger we are as a result. When I was a kid I thought I was vulnerable. And a lot of the time, I *was*. But I was actually already a lot tougher than I imagined. I'd kept going right through the time after my father died and we'd moved to France, even though there were definitely times when all I wanted was to go back to my old life in England.

And yet I ended up loving my time in France. I really thrived. I even joined a local football academy and was thinking about becoming a professional footballer. Then, when I hit my mid-teens I realised that I was desperate to explore more of the world. I'd had all the adventures I could in that pretty, quiet corner of Normandy, and it was time to leave. That's what led to me joining the British Army when I was seventeen.

Two decades on I still remember what a huge culture shock it was to exchange rural France for the uncompromising environment of the army's training centre. The soldiers I met couldn't get their heads round how polite and nice I was. When they weren't taking the piss out of my French accent and Gallic mannerisms, they were looking at me like I was some strange animal that had just stepped out of a zoo.

'Jesus,' I'd think to myself in the few moments I had to myself. 'What the hell have I done?' Suddenly my family seemed very far away. Was this the right decision?

The excitement and enthusiasm I'd had about the idea of joining the army melted away and was replaced by a little voice inside my head saying, 'You can quit. Just turn around and retrace your footsteps. You can give up. Nobody will mind.' I began to feel overwhelmed. There's very little in life as crushing as seeing what you thought was your perfect dream turn into a total nightmare before your eyes. The little voice got bigger. So too did the temptation to quit. I knew I'd be able to slot straight back into the life I'd left behind. Everything that I'd been so sick of just a couple of weeks ago now seemed to shine with promise.

I don't know why, but one day I had a sudden flash of memory. I thought back to my first experience of France almost a decade earlier – the searing, almost blinding emotional pain that followed losing my father, and the shock of being snatched out of my happy, comfortable life in Portsmouth. There was the first day at a new school in a new country, with all the kids laughing at me because I was so clearly lost and bewildered.

And yet I'd managed to survive. And I was even stronger now. I'd coped with all of that shit back then, so why was I so intimidated by what I was facing now? This memory was a game-changer for me. I genuinely felt a couple of inches taller. The next time we went out on a run I was faster than I'd ever been before. All the stuff I was struggling with was put into perspective. Yes, it was hard and uncomfortable. But that's true of so many experiences. The fact that something is difficult isn't a good enough reason to stop doing it. Often, I've found, the stuff that's most challenging is also the most worth persisting with.

That's the approach I've tried to take right through my life. At those moments when I've been at my lowest ebb, when I hear that whisper telling me, 'Just give up, quit, it'll be easier,' I take a few seconds to remind myself of how much I am capable of and how much I've already achieved.

You can do the same. Next time you're on the verge of quitting something because you think it's too painful, or you worry you're not going to be able to cope, think back to all the tricky things you've already survived. Think back to all the challenges you've seen off. Think back to all the hard times you've endured. It might be that you'll remember a skill you employed that helped you win through, or it might be that you can draw strength from reminding yourself exactly how resilient, how strong, you really are.

In some ways that's the ultimate plot twist. The hero that you look to for inspiration when you're struggling isn't a sportsperson, a soldier, a great figure from history, or even somebody off the telly.

It's you.

UNTIL YOUR LAST BREATH

I've been asked by people suffering from serious illness how they can maintain hope. I tell them that the only thing I know that even vaguely compares to their situation is combat. My attitude when I was in uniform was always the same. Never end the fight. Keep battling until your last breath. And when that comes, you probably won't know about it. That's how it was. You wouldn't have given up. You wouldn't have ended the fight, the fight will have ended you. If when I was on tour I caught one in the head, would I know about it? Would I fuck!

That fight, that determination to never let yourself get beat, is a thread that runs through the stories of so many of the most awe-inspiring people I've met. In the military it was triple amputees or guys who were shot in the lungs. They believed, and they came through it. No matter the odds, they didn't stop believing that they'd win that battle.

Or there's the man I know who struggled against cancer for years. Treatment after treatment failed, and then one worked. 'Never give up,' he told me, a big smile on his face. He understood that if you're willing to keep going, even if you feel as if you're just clinging on, then you're giving yourself a chance of winning.

It's only when you give up that you *know* it's all over. In the meantime, every extra breath you take is an opportunity to make progress. Every extra breath is another victory. Because you're still alive. You're still going.

NO REGRETS?

I believe in trying to lead a life with as few regrets as possible. One of the most straightforward ways of doing this is to make sure that I don't become a man who quits as soon as the going gets tough. Quitting can become a habit. You do it once, and then you find that next time it gets a bit easier. The time after that it's easier still. Before you know it, you've established a way of life whose parameters are defined by your weakness rather than your strength.

Every time you give something up, you're adding another regret to the pile. Eventually the weight of all of those lost opportunities, all of those half-finished plans, all of those abandoned ambitions, will begin to crush you. That's certainly what Jack experienced. Is that really what you want too?

FAIL TO PREPARE, PREPARE TO FAIL

You have to be prepared for pain. You cannot afford to let it surprise you. If you go into something just telling yourself that it's going to be sweetness and light from beginning to end then you're denying some of the most basic facts about life.

Sometimes bad things do happen. You can't stop that. But you can try to do the sort of mental preparation needed to ensure that, when everything goes south, you're not caught completely unawares. Because if you're not mentally ready for the bad times that will inevitably strike, then you're going to be far more vulnerable to the temptation to give up.

That's why, when I signed up to go on tour, I forced myself to acknowledge that some of my friends probably wouldn't come back. And I reminded myself over and over that there was at least a possibility I might sustain a serious injury. I made sure that this knowledge was programmed into my head.

There were guys in the Marines who had that mentality of 'It's never going to be me.' Well, really? You're not going on a big lads' holiday, you're going to war. You've got to understand what it is you've signed up for. Don't pretend that there won't be consequences just because you can't face up to that reality.

And guess what? When we did start to take casualties, it was the men who'd pretended to themselves that they were off on a sort of heavily armed road trip that really suffered. The reality of the situation hit them so much harder than it would have if they'd taken the time to get their heads straight in advance.

I find it also helps if you remind yourself that every bit of pain you take now will make you stronger in the long run. In my last book, *Mental Fitness*, I talked about how you can get across the pain threshold. What I should have said is that what is true for physical suffering is actually just as true for mental suffering. Once you've gone through it, things *will* get better. The next time you push yourself, you'll experience less pain. Go again and there will be even less pain. Eventually, you'll be numbed to it.

GRIND IT OUT

People want instant gratification. They want the reward without the work. The problem is: that's not life. Good things don't come from shortcuts or magic tricks. In my world, there's no such thing as a life hack. You have to commit to a process. You have to be in it for the duration.

It's entirely possible that the first time you try something new you'll struggle. You might even fail. That's OK. That's absolutely normal. Do your best to find out what went wrong and what you could do better in the future. Try again. You'll probably get a bit closer this time, and you'll learn a bit more. Try again. At some point, you'll get there. That was the big mistake that Jack made. He didn't realise that just because you fail once, it doesn't mean that you'll fail for ever.

At the beginning of my military career I really struggled with any exercise that involved putting weight on my back. When I could run unencumbered I'd always be at the front, but load me up with 30kg and I'd fall behind everyone. It was so dispiriting, and the worst of it was that it was all unfolding in public. Two years in, one of the NCOs suggested I should quit.

That made something click in my head: someone telling me I should quit after two years of hard effort made me want to succeed even more, and literally overnight it all changed. The next time we went out with heavy Bergens I was near the front of the group.

So that's why I always say to people, you've just got to keep at it. A lot of people give up at the first, second or third hurdle – they drop out of the queue and try something else, then five years down the line they realise they never should have given up and join the back of the queue again. It's all about having the perseverance to stick at something through the good and the bad.

Ignore people who complain that 'It's going to be a long road.' What the fuck do they expect? Life *is* a long road. Most people are on this planet for decades. I'm forty-one as I write this, so if I live until I'm a hundred I've got another sixty years. Don't think about time. Don't think about your destination. Think about the next positive step you can take. Do it increment by increment. Commitment by commitment. Prove to yourself that you know what perseverance and dedication mean. Graft and graft and graft if you need to. And remember that nothing worth anything comes easily. Look back at your life. You didn't fluke any of the stuff you're proud of – you worked for it. If you didn't put the hours in, you wouldn't value the prize in the same way.

My boy Gabriel was disappointed about having been put in the lowest set for maths. But if and when he gets put up to set two, he is going to feel so much better for having worked his way there than if he'd started out higher up.

He'll know he's earned his place. He'll know that he deserves it and so won't be looking over his shoulder all the time worrying that he's not good enough.

There's probably only 1 per cent of the population who smash whatever they do. Good luck to them! The rest of us have to start somewhere further down the ladder, and some will be right at the bottom. I wouldn't want to start at the top. I wouldn't want to be one of those people who gets dealt all the best hands by life. Because where, realistically, can they go with that? What can they achieve and say to themselves: I built that. I shed blood, sweat and tears, but I built that?

EXERCISE
MAKE DIFFICULTY A FEATURE, NOT A BUG

It's so easy to avoid things that are difficult. In fact, it's so easy that it becomes a habit that's tough to break. It gets to the point when you find yourself in the sort of rut where you never try anything new or challenging because you're always telling yourself, 'It's too hard, I won't be any good at it.'

But hard isn't the same as impossible. And there's no shame in finding something difficult. That just means you're stretching yourself. You're becoming a better version of you!

More than that, I think it's wrong to assume that difficulty is inherently a negative thing. We forget that we probably found a lot of the things we enjoy and take for granted now really tricky and intimidating to begin with. We also forget that the process of working something out that *seems* challenging can actually be incredibly rewarding. Think how satisfying it is to finally master a tricky skill. You can feel your neurons firing and it leaves you exhilarated.

One thing you can try to do is change your relationship with difficulty. Instead of seeking ways to avoid it, why not actually hunt difficulty out?

If there's a steep hill on your way home from work that you'd usually cycle around, why not try to cycle up it? It's likely that the first time you give it a go, you'll struggle. You might even have to get off and push your bike after just a few metres, but that doesn't matter – next time you'll probably be able to get a bit further, and eventually, after much effort, you'll reach the top in one go.

The important thing is that if you come to see your fear of difficulty as a mental block that you can challenge, you'll no longer be dodging stuff because it's a bit awkward. You're growing your world and embracing new experiences.

LESSONS

- When you quit too easily you're just piling up regrets for the future. Don't let a minute's relief be the prelude to a lifetime's pain.

- Whenever you find yourself struggling and tempted to give up, use your own past as an inspiration. Remind yourself instead of what you're capable of. Remind yourself how resilient you are, how many problems you've overcome, how many solutions you've come up with.

- Don't make yourself vulnerable to the temptation to quit by failing to anticipate potential problems. The more you prepare for the possibility of bad things happening, the better you'll be able to respond when they do.

- If something is hard work, that very often means it's worth persisting with. The achievements we value most, the achievements we are most proud of, are almost always those we've worked hardest for. Nobody has ever been given a gold medal for something that's just fallen into their lap.

- Don't shy away from difficult or complex things. Not only are they more rewarding once you've completed them – you'll learn so much more from failing at something that challenged you than you ever would from succeeding at something you found piss-easy.

CHAPTER 8

YOU'RE NOT SETTING YOURSELF HIGH ENOUGH STANDARDS

MAYBE THERE ARE other lads that have made a more catastrophic first impression in the SBS than I did. Maybe. But I very much doubt it.

The people who were still standing at the end of Selection all got a coach down to get badged. I was just about hanging in there, coming to terms with one of the worst hangovers of my life. In fact, I think I was probably still pissed. The night before, we'd been invited into the Sergeants' Mess. Finally, we could let ourselves go after months of being pushed to our limits. The alcohol – and there had been a lot of it – had ripped through our tired, elated bodies. I was giddy halfway through my first pint. It would have been a memorable evening, except … I wasn't sure I could recall much of it.

We all got off the coach at the barracks. What we were supposed to do next was catch another coach that'd take us to the place where we'd be given our badges. Seven of us managed that simple task. One of us didn't. Unfortunately, that one was me.

We'd been told that we were OK to leave our bags on the first bus, so I'd done that. But as we were walking to the next coach, which was on the other side of the camp, someone chirped up to remind us that we needed our berets. 'Shit,' I thought, 'I've left mine in my bag.'

I still had a Marine's mentality then. This sort of thing felt really important. I wasn't yet that chilled, bearded SF guy cutting about. My mindset was freshly shaven and ramrod-straight. I didn't want to get balled out for my stupidity, so I sprinted back to the coach, retrieved my beret and then did my best to catch up the others. But as I ran up and down the camp's streets, it became increasingly clear that not only had I lost track of rest of the guys, I also had very little idea of where I needed to get to if I wanted to catch the coach that was due to leave any minute. I glanced down at my watch. Fuck. My face reddened, I could feel sweat trickling down my back and my heart bouncing around in my chest.

The panic seemed to make my hangover's symptoms even more severe. My mouth was dry, my stomach churned and it seemed as if a blacksmith had taken up residence in my brain. Fuck. It was becoming increasingly hard to think clearly. My mind was a blur of featureless accommodation blocks. Up the main straight. I tried another couple of avenues, but got the same result. Jesus, had I just run past the NAAFI again? Where was I?

I was sure that the coach would have left by now. I couldn't believe what was happening. I'd made my way through dense, unmappable jungles. I'd hiked through the Brecon Beacons, navigating through the worst weather that the mountains could throw at me, and now I'd got lost in a fucking *camp*? An unpleasant series of self-recriminations began to cycle through my mind. Why did I go out last night? Why didn't I spend more time sorting out my kit? What had I done?

Suddenly I had the horrible realisation that my future in the Special Forces might be hanging in the balance. We'd just been through an unforgiving, brutally unsentimental process. One officer was failed on the very last day. He'd had to walk past as the rest of us were shaping our berets. I began to worry that my fuck-up was going to give people a reason to change their mind about me. Was I going to have to watch other people being badged while I was condemned to slink back to my unit with my tail between my legs?

Five minutes passed, then ten, then twenty. It was just as I was about to give in to the temptation to find a nice cool corner of the base and crawl into it that a guy dressed casually in a T-shirt, jeans and hiking boots stopped me.

'All right, mate? You look a bit lost. Can I help?'

I took in his long hair, sideburns and the easy, relaxed way he held himself. I knew straightaway that he was in the SBS.

Trying to keep my voice level, even as panic was bouncing around every cell of my body, I explained that I'd just passed Selection and was trying to find the coach that was supposed to take me off to my badging ceremony.

To my relief he seemed to know what I was talking about. 'You guys are doing down to get your berets?'

'Yes!'

We were walking side by side at a slouchy pace. Inside I was screaming *run, run, run*.

'Were you out last night?'

I gave him a bleary look.

He began to look amused. 'The coach left ten minutes ago.'

My heart sank. My first day at the squadron. Oh my God.

He smiled. 'You better get down there.'

'It's my first time here. I don't know where anything is.'

The smile was still there. 'I'll drive you.'

Without much ceremony, and without going any faster, we strolled down and he grabbed a vehicle. 'Jump in.'

'Thanks, staff.'

As I settled myself in the seat he held his hand out to me: 'Gaz, not staff. What are you, ex-Marine?'

'Yeah, but I was in the Engineers before that.'

'Ex-Engineer? You're coming to my squadron.'

It seemed to be getting worse. It wasn't just that I'd made myself look a numpty in front of another SBS soldier, he was someone I was actually going to be serving under.

Then, casually, he said, 'We're going out in two weeks.'

While I was taking this in, he spoke again. 'What's your name?'

'Middleton.'

'Middleton. You're with me. You finished right at the top of your Selection group, didn't you?'

He squinted at me, as if he didn't quite believe what he'd just said. And who could blame him? What must this guy think of me? He never stopped being friendly, but I could see that part of him was wondering, 'Who is this liability? How did he slip through the net?'

My thoughts began to spiral. I kept trying to remind myself that not only had I passed Selection, but I'd been one of the best performers in my cohort. And yet here I was getting lost in a barracks. Maybe I'd just got lucky? Did I really deserve to be here?

Twenty minutes later, he'd caught up with the coach and I was back on track. Once the ceremony started, one thing became very clear. I'd never actually needed my beret ...

NORMALLY WHEN YOU pass Selection you get a couple of months off because your body and mind need a chance to heal. But, as Gaz had warned me, fourteen days later I was doing pre-deployment training.

'No matter what they think of me now,' I told myself, 'I'm going to show them on the ground.'

I set myself the highest standards I could and worked like a demon to meet them. As a result I smashed it, absolutely flying through that training phase. I was so quick, so skilful. When I came out the other side I'd been appointed point man – a role that's usually only given to people with far more experience under their belt.

Going out so quickly was the best thing that could have happened to me. It was the chance to show them I wasn't the goof that my fuck-up might have suggested I was. Nobody ever mentioned what had happened back in Poole or suggested that it had changed their opinion of me, although the fear that they might do so remained there in my head. I didn't want to give the Special Forces any indication at all that their new recruit wasn't up to the job. I didn't want to look back and think, 'Phew, I got lucky there.' I wanted to be able to stare in the mirror and know that I'd earned my place.

What I also understood was that there was no question of lowering my standards once I'd got my feet under the table. Throughout all the years I served, I never let up. Not once. And I've carried exactly the same attitude into my life beyond the military, because I know that if you ever let yourself get complacent, if you approach everything with a 'Will this do?' attitude, then you're guaranteeing that at some point sooner or later you'll find yourself trapped behind the wall.

You don't need to be an elite soldier to possess an elite soldier's mentality. Whatever you're involved in, you should be demanding as much of yourself as you possibly can. High standards enable you to achieve your goals. They help keep you motivated. They form the bedrock of your growth as an individual. If you don't go into projects, or jobs, or relationships wanting to excel, why embark on them in the first place?

YOU SET THE STANDARDS

Who sets your standards? There's only one right answer: you. You should never need to be told what standards are expected of you. You should be setting them yourself.

When you set your standards high and aim to hit them consistently, then you'll always be kept on your toes. OK should never be good enough. That's the way that the best athletes approach their sport. Cristiano Ronaldo was born with outrageous talent. And yet it's his unbelievable commitment that stands out. He works and works and works and works. He's relentless in what he asks of himself. He knows that there's no progression, no success, without struggle.

Do you want to look back on your life twenty years on and be cursing the fact that you let an opportunity slip through your fingers because you were too complacent, too lazy to make the most of it?

I'll keep hammering this point again and again, but honesty is just so important when it comes to setting your standards. *You* know if you've done well or not. *You* know when you've made a positive dent in the world. It doesn't matter how other people respond. You have to be content that *you* have performed to the standards you expect of yourself. If you know in your heart of hearts that you could have done better at a particular job if you'd actually put your back into it, then you should treat any praise you get as a result of that work as irrelevant. Equally, if you've fucked up because you did a sloppy job, you shouldn't be reassured when somebody says, 'Don't worry about it, I know you did your best.' This attitude is guaranteed to make your standards drop. This slippage might be imperceptible at first, but if you let it go on for long enough it becomes irreversible.

The opposite of the above is just as true. If you've put your heart and soul into something, if you know that you've done it to the best of your abilities, and then somebody shows up and dismisses it, don't give their opinion even a moment's attention. What they think in no way whatsoever diminishes the value of your achievement.

Complacency is success's deadliest enemy. You should never feel as if you've done enough. You should never tell yourself that you know everything. You should never risk taking time to pat yourself on the back, because if you do you'll find yourself sliding backwards and everything you've worked so hard for will have been thrown away. Your standards should never waver or diminish. If anything, the demands you place on yourself should only go one way: up.

The more you learn, the more you fail, the more resilient you become, the more you should be capable of. Keep raising the bar!

BETTER THAN IT NEEDS TO BE

Something one of my book editors once said has really stuck with me. It was in the early stages of putting together *First Man In*, when we were discussing our ambitions for the book. He looked me straight in the eye and said, 'I want it to be better than it needs to be.'

'What do you mean?'

'Well, lots of books by people who've got a platform like yours are just contractual exercises. Everyone involved puts the minimum work in, and often that's enough to sell enough copies to get it into the bestseller list and make everyone happy. But I think we can do more. A lot more. I want you to produce a book that's better than it needs to be, because that's what keeps readers coming back for more. That's what makes readers tell their mates about the book.'

And so that's exactly what we did. We worked our arses off to make something that everyone was really proud to put out into the world. I wanted people who picked it up to realise how important writing books was to me. That was true then, and it's still true now.

EXCELLENCE, DAY IN, DAY OUT

I talk to lots of businesses about what they can do to change or improve their culture. Almost always the moment comes when we starting talking about professionalism. What does it mean to be a good professional? What can individuals do to become more professional, and how can institutions create environments that encourage and support professional behaviour?

People tend to throw a lot of buzzwords and jargon at me when we start that conversation. (What the fuck does a 'synergised implementation strategy' even *mean*?) Or they'll go for big concepts, like 'radical candour' or whatever.

The upshot of all this is that they're surprised when I start talking about consistency. Because, let's be honest, it's not a very sexy idea. As far as I'm concerned, however, consistency is the foundation of any success. Can you do the basics to a very high standard consistently? It doesn't matter to me if you can occasionally pull it out of the bag if most of the time you fall short. What's important is that you can do it every single day. This is what trips a lot of people up. They can sometimes perform to the standard required, but they can't do it consistently. They don't have the requisite discipline or motivation.

The importance of being consistent was rammed down our throats on Selection. Ultimately, it was what helped sort out those who were capable of getting through the course from those who weren't.

The hill phase gets rid of the dead wood: the guys who are just there for the kudos or those who simply aren't up to it. You're carrying extreme weights over an extreme distance, the weather's disgusting and the days start earlier than you can imagine. A handful of people make it through. The vast majority don't.

After that you're out for even more training. There's a relentless series of exercises that can come at any time. This is to see how you operate under extreme pressure when you're also at the limits of your fatigue. The moment you get that single tick indicating you're guilty of an error, you're off the course. During this stage more and more are cut away, more often than not as the result of errors made by being tired and stressed.

It's full-on for months. Out of the hundreds of people who started the course I participated in, there were only a handful left at the end. It's all designed to ensure that those who do pass are men that the unit knows it can rely on to perform at a consistently high level whatever the circumstances.

This is what you should be aiming to do. Make every day a good day. Be the sort of person that other people trust because they know that they can always rely on you. And of course, consistency isn't just important in the workplace. You need to be a consistent parent, partner, daughter or brother. You can't afford to decide to be a great parent only on the days when it suits you.

THE MISTAKE

I realise I've made Selection seem like the most brutal, yet also most efficient, recruitment system in history. Some people did slip through the net, however. For whatever reason, they'd been given an opportunity that they didn't quite deserve. Sometimes, when there are concerns about manpower, the CO steps in and allows someone through who in other circumstances would have been bombed-out. They get given the benefit of the doubt.

We could be unforgiving and harsh in those situations. There'd always be someone who took one of these lads aside and said, 'How the *fuck* did you pass? What are *you* doing *here*?' What was really telling, though, was how they responded to that question. Some saw it as a challenge that they needed to rise to. They were desperate to prove that they were worthy of that lucky break. Others crumbled. I've seen people who've been absolutely destroyed by the pressure.

It wasn't as if we were in the management team in a mid-sized accounting firm where somebody had fluked into a job. What's the worst thing that's going to happen there? Numbers in the wrong column? In the SBS you weren't just risking our lives, you were risking your own. I don't want to be dragging your carcass off the battlefield and delivering it to your wife and kids in a box. Mate, do us a favour, do your family a favour, do *yourself* a favour and accept that this isn't for you.

But as much as we hated it, those free passes enraged the instructors even more.

The lads that did well on Selection get an arm round their shoulders. Those that didn't, the people who scrape through or get given a CO's pass, are given short shrift. I still remember now watching a guy come into the Sergeants' Mess a couple of steps behind me on the night we were finally invited into their inner sanctum. He was high off the buzz of being admitted to the elite of the elite. That buzz did not last.

One of the SAS instructors turned round and saw him. 'Get out. You shouldn't even be here. Have a drink and then fuck off.'

He came up to me looking bewildered. 'Ant, I've been told to get out.' He seemed shaken and uncertain, as if he couldn't quite work out if he was the victim of a cruel practical joke. I could feel something imploring in his voice, like he wanted me to reassure him that there had been a misunderstanding, that everything would be OK.

The thing was, I knew he was shit. I knew he didn't deserve to be here. It was a mystery that he'd made it through the jungle phase. And every mistake he made in the weeks that followed – after a while we just stopped counting – left us even more mystified. Each time he got picked up on something, I'd thought to myself, 'They're going to bin him,' and I was fairly sure that's what the instructors had wanted to do. And yet here he was, about to join the SBS.

'Just go now, mate. Do yourself a favour, don't even finish your drink. You're getting badged tomorrow. You'll be fine. He's SAS, you probably won't even see him again. Just do what you've got to do.'

Pretty much from the day he joined the unit this guy got called 'the Mistake'. That was his challenge. It was up to him to prove to us that we were the ones who'd made the big error.

If somebody tells you that you're not good enough, or that you're not ready, it's on you to respond. The first step is to be brutally honest with yourself. If what they're saying to you is true, then great, you know what you need to do to the required standard. If you're passionate enough you'll push yourself and get there. By contrast, if you genuinely think they're wrong, then brilliant, you can show them that they've made a mistake, and you can use everything they've said to you as fuel to motivate yourself.

That didn't happen with the Mistake. He was a complete cluster-fuck. It wasn't just a question of skill. The application and effort weren't there either. It was like he was so deflated by the abuse he got that he struggled to locate his motivation. Or maybe he just thought that the fact that he'd got into the SBS – fluke or not – was enough, and that he didn't have to try anymore. Either way, something that he had probably dreamed of for years slipped through his fingers. In the process, he lost the respect of the sort of men whose opinion he valued most. So, whatever you do, don't be that guy who drags everybody else down with them. When life hands you an opportunity, work as hard as you possibly can to show the world that you deserve it. Work as if your life depended on it. Don't be complacent. Don't be lazy. Don't live your life on default, hoping that you'll get another lucky roll of the dice. Don't be like the Mistake.

ASK YOURSELF HARD QUESTIONS

Elon Musk, the world's richest man, has got to where he is by asking really fucking ambitious, uncomfortable big questions of himself. Sometimes he gets the right answer, sometimes he doesn't.

It doesn't matter if you don't become a space-rocket-building tech billionaire, you can still approach your life in that way. In fact, on one level you probably already are. At a cellular level, we're asking ourselves difficult questions and providing complex answers all of the time. If you were aware of all the things your body was doing just to keep you upright, let alone what it did to help you cross the room, it would send you absolutely crackers. Your mind would just not be able to cope.

Luckily, you don't have to think much about those things. And yet it is absolutely worth asking yourself hard questions. Be bold. Be imaginative. Don't be afraid to creep up to the outer limits of what you think is plausible. Can I really make that business idea work? How would I go about retraining as a therapist?

Then it's up to you to try to find solutions. You might find them, you might not, but I know one thing: whatever the outcome, you'll learn a fuck of a lot along the way. You might even have fun.

LESSONS

- The Special Forces demand the highest possible standards. I carried that attitude right through my time in the SBS, and it's still something I insist on to this day. If you don't want to end up trapped behind the wall, you should do the same.

- Consistency is key. I don't give a fuck if you can turn it on when you feel like it. You have to perform at the same level day after day after day.

- You and you alone should be the person setting your standards. You should have absolutely zero interest in performing at a level that satisfies other people – you should be performing at a level that satisfies you. Everything else is irrelevant.

- Don't ever think that doing just enough is good enough. Don't ever be happy with doing the bare minimum. Make sure that everything you do is better than it needs to be.

- If you're committed to growing and becoming the best version of yourself, then what's good enough for you today probably won't be good enough in five years. Your expectations of yourself should grow as time goes on.

- When somebody tells you that you're not good enough, you have a choice. You can either shrink into yourself and confirm their first, negative impression of you, or you can prove them wrong. Make sure you always take that second option. What better motivation could you ask for?

CHAPTER 9

YOU'RE TOO AFRAID TO MAKE DECISIONS

I KNEW ABBY through friends of friends. As often happens with new people you meet, we got chatting at a party. She told me that she and her partner hadn't been happy for a long time. I was a bit surprised that she'd revealed something so personal to somebody she'd only just met.

'Don't worry,' she laughed, 'trust me, the state of mine and Tom's relationship is very much not a secret. Ask anyone in this room. They've all heard it all.'

They'd met young, she said, had two kids quickly, and it was only when things had settled down a bit that they discovered they had nothing in common, apart from the children that they both loved dearly. They lived pretty separate lives now. When they did spend any time together, which wasn't often, they were at each other's throats constantly.

'We're just different people,' she said, sounding resigned and sad. 'We're fundamentally incompatible, I don't really know how else to explain it. I'm just so torn between not wanting to chuck everything away after all these years, and wanting to give myself the chance of starting again. Perhaps having another family with somebody else. Every time I try to work out what to do I feel my head start spinning. What happens if by trying to make things better, I just end up making things worse? And who's to say I'm going to be happier if I do leave Tom? I don't want to fucking die alone with cats for company, do I?'

She stopped talking. I could see she was looking at me, as if expecting something. Then it clicked. She wanted me to make her decision for her. She wanted someone else to tell her that she should either double down and try to fix what was left of her marriage, or get out while she still could.

'I can't give you what you need,' I told her, 'that's not my call to make. You know that, don't you?'

She looked disappointed, and nodded her head.

A LOT OF people are like Abby – they can't, or won't, make decisions. They are afraid of the consequences of getting a decision wrong, which very often simply means that they're afraid of being judged by others. And, a lot of the time, people just don't trust in themselves. They'll think about that new job they're considering applying for and end up asking themselves: Am I good enough? Do I know enough? Will I make a fool of myself?

Then the decision that lies before them stops looking like an opportunity and starts to feel like a burden. They slope their shoulders, hoping that somebody else will make the decision for them, or that some act of God will mean they don't have to make up their mind. All the while, their world is shrinking, their opportunities for growth and excitement are dwindling. They're always waiting, waiting. Then, all of a sudden, they find it's too late. And it's then, *only* then, that the ditherer turns round and says, 'Oh, I could have done that!'

Yeah? Maybe you could. Maybe you did have it in you. But the fact is, you didn't. The number one thing that ex-military people say to me is: 'I wish I'd gone on Selection. It's the biggest regret in my life.' I hear it again and again.

There's only one response to that: 'Well, why didn't you?'

I believe that every challenge you turn away from, every experience you avoid, makes your world shrink. When you don't commit to making a decision, you're depriving yourself of the chance to change and grow. You're ensuring that your world will stay for ever the same.

And it's when you stay still like that that you become vulnerable to stress, to anxiety. Doing nothing is not the safe option it might look like at first. Doing nothing means you cut yourself off from the chance to learn, evolve and change, to make mistakes, to embrace failure, to succeed. You're not allowing a process to occur that should be taking place within us all. You end up trapped behind a wall that *you* have built. And the danger is that this stasis becomes your norm.

But when you do have the confidence to make decisions, you don't live with regrets – even if you sometimes end up making the wrong call. There's nothing in my life I regret. Nothing. Everything, good or bad, has helped me and has formed part of my learning curve.

And the reason I don't have any regrets is because I've committed to everything I've done. When you commit, you're either going to get it right or you're going to get it wrong. I'd rather live my life learning from mistakes than I would being that person sitting on his sofa asking himself, 'What if?'

DON'T MAKE A MOUNTAIN OUT OF A MOLEHILL

One mistake so many of us make over and again is to cast decisions as being dramatic, set-piece events. But in truth, making our mind up is part of the texture of our lives. We make over 30,000 decisions a day. Over 200 of these are about food! You're so good at making decisions that most of the time you take them without even being aware of it.

What time to get out of bed? Should I leave five minutes early to beat the traffic? What route should I take? Shall I order a flat white or a cappuccino?

But we forget this when it comes to the so-called big decisions. We forget that the ability to choose one option or another is just like a muscle that we use over and over again. And so we make it harder than we need to because we build up its significance in our head. If you end up writing endless lists of pros and cons, you'll find yourself caught in a messy web of words and figures.

I know people who get so wrapped up in the stress of making a decision that it stops them ever doing stuff that would actually make them happier and healthier. Instead of taking positive action, they are paralysed by indecision – so much so that it even affects their sleep.

At the end of the day, making decisions is purely a psychological process. It demands nothing physical of you. Do I commit to this course of action? Yes or no. It's as simple as that. Then you make a start. Take a step. Take small chunks off the problem.

WHY YOU SHOULD NEVER BE AFRAID OF WHAT YOU DON'T KNOW

The other trap people fall into is waiting endlessly until they feel they know enough to be sure before they commit. But you're never going to have perfect knowledge of the future – which is precisely what makes it so exciting to me. The only way you'll ever find out what's going to happen is to commit and take the plunge, then soak up the consequences, whatever they may be.

Or you could choose the alternative, which is to do nothing and live with regret because once again life has rushed past and left you behind. Certainty only comes after it's already too late. The best decision-makers are those who have made their peace with the knowledge that none of us is ever going to be able to control every element in our messy, imperfect, exciting universe.

JUST DO IT!

Self-esteem and the ability to make decisions go hand in hand because a decision is a statement of faith in your abilities. It's a commitment to yourself and your future. I always believe that I can make something work. I go into every project confident that I'll be able to meet whatever challenges it throws up. It's this that underpins my decision-making.

But when you lack self-confidence – if you're the sort of person who has convinced yourself that everything you touch turns to shit so why even bother trying – you're always going to hesitate before making that crucial commitment.

Chapter 10, on p. 161, contains tips on how to build your self-belief. But I'd urge you to remember two things. The first is that you're probably much more capable than you're willing to admit. So why give up in advance? Why not give yourself the chance to find out how strong and competent you really are? After all, you don't win a race by giving up before the starting gun has been fired.

Another way to build confidence when it comes to making decisions is to simply do it. I've always believed that you've got to action stuff if you really want to understand it. I might want to walk along a gravel path in bare feet. But until I actually do it, I won't actually know whether I should be putting my weight on my toes or my heels. It's by actioning something that you come up with a solution.

And the more you commit to making decisions and dealing with their consequences, the easier they'll become. You'll realise how much better you feel knowing that instead of shirking the challenge and retreating that bit further into the darkness of your shell, you're making steady progress in the right direction.

You'll also realise that you have much less to lose than you think …

WHAT'S THE WORST THING THAT COULD HAPPEN?

The worst thing in the world when you're in combat is a leader who is incapable of making decisions. Even a bad decision is almost always better than no decision. The same is true of life in civvy street.

If you make a decision and it doesn't work, then that's a shame, of course, but you now know a hell of a lot more than you did five minutes, or a day, ago. You know that a particular technique doesn't work, that an option is off the table. You've taken another step closer to finding the solution.

A job or a relationship doesn't work out? That can be truly unpleasant, but at least you know that that company or that person wasn't for you – not everything and everyone is! And now you're not going to go to your grave wishing you'd given it a go.

An experience might be positive, it might be negative. That shouldn't matter to you. What's important is that you've had that experience. And it's now up to you to make something positive out of it.

Ultimately, when you make a decision you're engaging more fully with the world around you. You're putting yourself out there. You're giving yourself a chance. You're opening yourself up to opportunities. So even if you make the wrong decision, or if whatever it is you end up deciding to do has some unintended consequences, you're putting yourself in a position to grab something good for yourself.

That probably means taking risks and opening yourself up to failure. And that probably also means that people will talk about you. Good. You're doing something. But think of all the things that will pass you by if you don't step out of the door.

EXERCISE
A FRIEND IN NEED

When you're agonising about a decision, ask yourself what advice you'd give a friend in your position. It's really clarifying to be able to adopt a different perspective. I bet nine times out of ten you'd tell them to go for it, wouldn't you? You'd explain how important it was that they went ahead and pursued the opportunity to get promoted that had just come up at their firm; and you'd probably be far more confident when it came to telling them to leave a relationship that was no longer making them happy. You might even point out how regretful they'd be if they didn't. Why not adopt the same approach to your own life?

Who are you making the decision for anyway?

The thought of what other people might think looms too large in most human beings' decision-making. We're so quick to say to ourselves, 'What will the other people in my office say if I do x or y, or I get that call wrong? I've got to work with them.'

I've talked about how to overcome the fear of other people's judgement in Chapter 5. But what I want to say here is that if you're letting the thought of what your mum, your mates or your colleagues *might* say if you make a particular decision cloud your thinking, then you're asking yourself the wrong questions.

You're not making the decision for them, you're making it for YOU. So why should you give a fuck what they think or say?

Think of Christopher Columbus, a great example of the good that can come from someone getting a decision *really* fucking wrong. He transformed his failure to discover a new route to India into something that changed the course of history. Because he committed to it. You don't know where your decision is going to take you. But you sure as hell know where not taking a decision will take you: nowhere.

DON'T SWEAT THE SMALL STUFF!

You could be the sort of person who does a million hours of research every time you buy a new kettle. Or you could accept that whichever one you buy will probably do a good enough job, and that there probably isn't a 'perfect' kettle out there. It's fair to say that there almost certainly isn't one that's worth the agonising decision-making process you've forced yourself to go through.

Some decisions are important. Most aren't. So don't waste your energy agonising over stuff that *really* doesn't matter. If you make every decision into a psychodrama, you're not only going to increase your stress – you'll also start to feel less in control of your existence.

THE MAGNET

The more you learn to trust your instincts, the more confident you'll become when it comes to making decisions. In fact, you'll barely be aware of the process of making your mind up at all.

One of the first things I say to people who come to me saying that they've hit a wall is this. Where is your energy taking you? What do you feel drawn to? The answer has to come from you. People can guide you. They can give you all the help in the world. But only you really have the answers. Only you know, when you take that first footstep, whether it feels right or wrong.

I always know when I've hit a wall. I can feel that change. My body seems to vibrate with impatience. I'm like a nail being dragged across a table by a magnet. There's a voice inside me going: 'It's time for something new. It's time for something new.'

Then I know that it's time to connect to that energy and find out what it is I need to do next. It's up to me to try to decipher what's going on, otherwise there's a chance of a missed opportunity. Somebody else will charge in and leave me wondering what could have been. I don't want to be one of those people who reach the end of their lives loaded down with regrets.

I trust myself because I've committed so often. I've done it so many times that I'm confident that I'll always be able

157

to figure it out. My television career could fall to pieces. I might never sell another book. Of course I'd be disappointed – I love what I do – but you better believe I'd find something else. It might not come immediately. I might have to search for a while; there might be a few false starts. But it's gonna come.

Then, when you find it, you have to commit. Go all in.

When you commit to yourself, everything else will follow. Whether it works out or not, you'll learn something. And when you learn, you grow. 'It hasn't worked out, but I'm so glad I gave myself the chance to find out. Now I know I can go forward without any regrets.'

You can steam forward, knowing you're not going to get demoralised by low self-esteem, jealousy, envy.

If, when you're thinking about committing to something, you feel uncomfortable, then that's a good sign. It means that you're being pulled towards it. And while nobody likes the sensation of being pulled around – because we all like to feel as if we're in control – you must not ignore that energy. Now that I'm familiar with that feeling, I recognise it as a sign that whatever is causing it is something that I should probably take a look at.

I wonder whether the same was true for Christopher Columbus. We think his big decision was whether to travel around the world. But that's not true. He already *knew* what he wanted to do. He didn't have to agonise about it or write a list of pros and cons. He was being pulled towards that journey. The only decisions he had to make were small ones: what sort of ships should we take? Who do I want to come with me? How much water do we need? How many provisions?

If you know yourself, if you have made the effort to connect with yourself, you will lead yourself to where you need to be.

THIS IS WHAT I explained to Abby while we were sipping our drinks at the party.

'The answer you're looking for,' I said, 'isn't outside you. I don't have it. That woman over there doesn't have it. It's not fucking floating around in the air above us. It's inside you. You're the only one who knows. You've got to find that answer – and then, when you've found it, commit to it. Commit to all the good and bad that your answer repre-sents, because there isn't going to be a perfect solution. There probably isn't going to be any solution to your situa-tion that doesn't involve pain. But if you just stay in an anguished state of mind for ever, you're going to drive your-self round the bend. It's not good for you, for your husband or your kids. Ask yourself what path you're being pulled towards. Then just take it. And don't look back.'

LESSONS

- You should never forget that every decision you duck is just a regret that you're storing up for later. You might think you've dodged something, but you're deceiving yourself. One day, that failure will bite you in the arse.

- Don't make decisions any harder than they need to be. Don't spend too much time agonising over consequences, don't draw up endless lists of pros and cons. Trust your instincts. If you think something is right, jump in.

- The consequences of not doing something are almost always worse than giving it a go. Even when a decision you take doesn't work out, there is so much you can learn from the experience. That failure will make you far stronger than hiding away on your couch ever could.

- So if you make the wrong call, don't worry too much – it's not the end of the world. But be humble. Be honest with yourself, and take any criticism you receive on board. Usually, when stuff goes wrong, you're left with a pretty clear idea of how you might do better next time. That's crucial information – don't ignore it.

- Don't get bogged down with anxiety over inconsequential decisions. Our lives are full of enough stress as it is, so why add to it?

CHAPTER 10

YOU DON'T BELIEVE
IN YOURSELF

TOO MANY PEOPLE spend their whole time on this planet telling themselves: 'I can't do that!'

When this becomes your mantra, you're basically giving up on life before you've even got started. These words – 'I can't do that!' – shrink your world and may prevent you from throwing yourself into challenging experiences that will enhance your existence because you're convinced you won't be able to cope with the stress. But here's the thing: you only need a spark of self-belief to change 'I can't do that!' into 'I can do that!' And that spark will come if you're willing to commit.

I REMEMBER ONE exchange I had with a woman who'd lost her mum four days before my tour rolled into her town.

The night she came I'd been speaking about commitment. 'Don't look at the journey in its entirety,' I'd said, 'because if you do that it'll look too much and you won't even put your foot on the bottom rung of the ladder. You won't commit. Instead, look to commit step by step. Make small, positive movements in the right direction. Each time you move forward, get used to the new space, then, when you're comfortable, take another step. Commit again, and again and again. Do it in your own time. Don't rush. Don't give yourself a deadline, because you'll just end up in a race against yourself.'

The example I gave them was the vehicle dunking drill from the Australian edition of *SAS: Who Dares Wins*. The contestant climbs into a Land Rover and fastens their seatbelt. The car is then lifted up and dumped into the water. As soon as it reaches the bottom and is fully submerged, the drill begins. The contestant needs to remove their seatbelt and leave the vehicle by an exit at its rear – we'd simulated the window having shattered. All in all, they're in there for forty to fifty seconds. Straightforward, but also a proper fucking challenge that asks as many questions of their mind as it does their body.

The important thing is that you don't panic once the vehicle has been dropped and starts filling up with water. If you take your seatbelt off then, before it's reached a stop, you'll just get pinned to the roof.

One of the other DSs demonstrated what the contestants needed to do. Now you've seen what you need to do, I told them, you need to remember that once the process starts, it doesn't stop. Who wants to step forward and go first?

Instantly one of the guys, Manu Feildel, stood up and took off his armband. He was done. This wasn't much of a surprise to me, as he'd already tried to VW at least once before. Fair enough.

Out of the corner of my eye I'd already seen Bonnie Anderson, one of the women. Her chin was down and I could see fear all over her face. She made a move to stand up too. She also wanted to hand her armband in.

'No,' I said. I was not having that. I knew that Manu was done, but with Bonnie it was different. She was just petrified by this particular challenge because she had a phobia of drowning.

I took her to one side away from everyone else and said, 'Look, I can tell this is one of your biggest fears, but I can't let you quit. You're looking at this task in its entirety and that's overwhelming. Unsurprisingly your fight-or-flight response is in overdrive and all you want to do is to get out of here. What I'm going to do is break all of this down for you into manageable bits. I just want you to go through a small series of commitments. I don't expect you to commit to the end. All I ask is for you to go as far as you can.

'Your first commitment is to get in the vehicle, sit down and put your seatbelt on. Nothing more. You don't need to think about what happens after that.'

She did this, no problem. I waited until she was ready.

'Now we're going to lift you up, then you'll be submerged in the water, and the drill will begin. *However*, the driver's-side window will be open. That's the sort of thing you should be observing anyway. When you make that first commitment, observe everything. Try not to let any detail escape you. Don't seize up.

'If you start to panic, you can just undo your seatbelt and escape through the window. Although, if you do that, you will fail the course.'

I wasn't worried about whether or not she'd fail that task – a lot of people would fail – all I wanted was to see her commit.

'That's another little commitment out of the way. If you can stay in, then wait, wait, wait, until the car finally reaches the bottom. Then take your seatbelt off and get out of the back. You'll have completed the task. Are you ready to commit to these stages?'

'Yeah,' she said, 'I can get in the vehicle.'

A start. A commitment. That was enough for me.

She got in and I made her try taking the seatbelt off a couple of times. I wanted her to see what it was like, and for her to see that this was one element she'd already mastered. When we were both happy, she put her hands on the steering wheel.

'Are you ready to commit to the next phase?'

She exhaled and looked unsure. 'I dunno, staff. I don't think I can.'

'Why not?'

'I feel as if I've hit the wall. I'm scared I'm going to panic.

What happens if I get caught on something and I can't get my seatbelt off?'

'But you've just shown me you can do that, no problem.'

'Yes, I can, quite happily.'

'So you've been through this first commitment phase and you know you're not going to get caught or snagged up. And remember what's on your right: the open window. Did you notice that?'

'No.' She was almost laughing at this.

'It's a big hole. Worst-case scenario, you can use it.'

She looked again. Then back to me. Then down at her seatbelt. Another deep breath.

'I'm ready to commit.'

'Good. Now don't burden your mind with bullshit and complication.'

She had a last burst of uncertainty. 'What if I get snagged? What if I panic?'

'You know neither of those things is going to happen. Just make one commitment at a time. Close your eyes, grab the steering wheel and clear your mind of all the bullshit you've just been spouting. Let me know when you're good to go.'

Twenty seconds passed. 'My mind's clear, staff.'

'Now, can you hold your breath for forty seconds? Once the vehicle lifts up, that's all you need to do. Ignore the crane, ignore the water, ignore everything else.'

'Yes, staff. Quite easily.'

'Good. You can do that. And you've already shown you can undo your seatbelt. So all you have left to do is swim two metres out of the back of the vehicle.'

Boom! You could see the change in her eyes immediately. That's what I love so much about this show.

I saw her, sitting cool as a cucumber as the vehicle was hoisted up and then slowly lowered into the water. She stayed calm as the water rose higher and higher, covering her belly, her chest, her neck, her chin, her mouth, her nose, then rising past her eyes. Still she did not flinch. When she felt the squeeze on her shoulder that told her that it was time to release, she continued to show the same almost otherworldly poise. When she slipped out of the belt and eased her way out of the back of the Land Rover, it was as if she had lived her whole life at the bottom of the sea.

When she emerged, her thumb raised in triumph, I knew something had changed inside her for ever.

Three days later, in the middle of the easiest, most innocuous task you can imagine, she quit, just as she'd threatened to before. This time, however, I knew that she really was at the end of her journey.

When I took her inside afterwards I asked her what was going on.

'I'm done, staff. I'm still so overwhelmed and happy after that water task. I don't need to complete the course in order for me to feel as if I've succeeded. That was my success. When I first saw that task, I never believed in a million years that I'd be able to do it. But when you broke it down like that, everything flipped. It's given me all the self-belief I ever needed.'

And if you look at her now, she is *flying*.

THE BIGGEST GIFT we can give ourselves is self-belief. It can't come from anybody else. It has to be you. It doesn't matter how many times other people tell you how wonderful you are – if you don't believe in yourself, then these are just empty words.

And self-belief comes from commitment. If you commit to something, even if you don't achieve your ultimate objective, then you're already on the way to success, because you've committed to yourself.

It's amazing what you learn by just committing once, for a few seconds. You start there, and God knows where that might lead to. The voice in your head that whispers, 'I can't do this, I can't do this,' gets transformed into one that shouts, 'I CAN DO IT! I CAN DO IT!'

There's no magic to any of this. All I did, all you have to do, is strip away everything that isn't real so that you're left with the actual tasks at hand. Don't fill your mind with apocalyptic scenarios. Don't think about every single worst-case scenario. That's all speculation, nothing more. These scenarios might, just might, exist at some point in the future, but they certainly fucking don't at this precise moment in your life. Instead, think about what is in front of you RIGHT NOW. Then commit to it. Simple as that.

The woman who messaged me after losing her mother said that this conversation about commitment was the main thing she took from my show. Before she'd left the house that evening she'd been involved in a complex and increasingly heated conversation with her two sisters. Because she was the eldest, her sisters wanted her to write and deliver their mother's eulogy. But she had told them point-blank that she couldn't do it. No way. Not in a million years. She had all of that ringing in her ears when she turned up at the venue.

The following morning she woke up with her mind full of everything I'd said about the commitment phase. She got up, went downstairs and repeated to herself something I'd said on stage the night before: 'Make that first commitment and see where it takes you.' Almost without knowing what she was doing, she grabbed paper and a pencil, put them on the table in front of her and sat down. She had no idea where she was going to go with it.

Until the pencil started moving on the paper she didn't even know what the first words were going to be. But once she started, she found that she could not stop. To begin with, she was pretty much just doodling: 'I love you, Mum, I miss you, Mum.' She filled a whole page, then looked at what she'd done. She ripped the page off, put it to one side, and asked herself: 'But why do I love you? Why do I miss you?'

Before she knew it, she'd filled another couple of pages. Twenty-four hours earlier, she'd thought she was incapable of writing a eulogy. Now she was holding one in her hand. At the moment she sent me the message, she was still unsure whether she'd be able to actually stand up and deliver it at the funeral. 'But I want to thank you, Ant,' she put in her message. 'That commitment phase really helped me. It really works. I used to think I couldn't write a eulogy. I've proved that I can. So although as I'm writing this I don't know whether I'll be able to speak these words in public, I'm beginning to think that that could change too.'

Whether or not she did give that eulogy, look how far she'd come in such a short time. Her experience reminded me of that part of *SAS Australia* I love the most. The moment usually arrives four or maybe five days in. It's when the recruits become aware of how much they've already changed. You can practically see them thinking, 'Wow, I didn't know I could do that. I've never felt that emotion before, but I've got through it, and it felt good.'

That's why I do the show. Not for the money or the fame or because I love being on TV, but because there's no better feeling than showing other people how amazing our bodies and minds are – and how much we're all capable of.

THE ARMOURY

A lot of people struggle with self-belief because they struggle with controlling their emotions. They feel as if they're at war with themselves. The powerful weapons in their emotional armoury that should be working on their behalf are actually turned against them.

This is something I talked about in great detail in my last book, *Mental Fitness*. If you want to be able to control your emotions, you have to be willing to expose them until you understand them completely.

You're never going to be able to expose them, however, if you live a risk-free life inside your comfort zone. So put yourself in situations that you know are going to provoke your emotions. Then, when an emotion wells up inside you, don't just let it float away. Grab it and study it. Work out precisely what it was that triggered you. How did that emotion manifest itself in you? Then do it again, and again, and again. Repetition is the key.

When you've exposed that emotion enough it will stop working against you, and start working for you.

That's what I did with the fear I experienced before and during combat. I kept on provoking it, again and again, walking that delicate line between life and death. To begin with I'd feel completely engulfed by terror, and it was just like one of those car crashes, with everything slowing down.

172

Then, when it was over, I almost couldn't believe I was still alive. I needed to get somebody to pinch me to check.

But after a while, after I'd ripped off layer after layer, I started to make the feeling of fear work for me. I'd burst into a room that I knew was full of enemy combatants and the fact that time slowed down now became an advantage. I started moving differently. Acting differently. Once I'd learned how to harness it, I became – paradoxically – more peaceful than at any other time in my life. I knew I was either going to die in that room, or walk out of it alive. There was no complication. It was the purest form of life. I experienced seconds filled with euphoria rather than paralysing fear.

But what frustrates me is that there isn't much incentive nowadays to expose and master your emotions in this way. I think it's because, if you can control your emotions, then it almost makes you self-sufficient. And society doesn't want that; it wants you to be reliant on the system. It wants you to feel as if you're a liability, that unless you suppress yourself you'll be an outcast. It wants to be able to say, 'Oh, he's on medication. He's no trouble now.'

This is why the media are always looking for signs of vulnerability in me. They keep coming and they keep coming. They want to find those chinks in my armour because they want me to be beholden to them. They want to be able to say, 'We can do something for you. Now you are reliant on us.'

THE ENEMY IN THE MIRROR

Too many of us are our own worst enemies. It's not exactly controversial to point out that if someone hates themselves, they're always going to struggle with confidence. If you don't think you deserve to be happy, you'll struggle to ever become the best version of yourself.

People who are really consumed with self-loathing often end up destroying healthy relationships, or putting a bomb under brilliant job opportunities because they don't feel as if they deserve them. If you think about yourself in those terms it's always going to have a profound physical effect. If you think you're shit then you'll feel like shit. It's such a heartbreaking thing to see in somebody else.

By contrast, when you start thinking of yourself as somebody who deserves to be happy and healthy, it'll transform your behaviour in subtle ways. You'll probably eat more healthily and take more exercise, because you'll have started to think of yourself as something valuable that needs to be taken care of. I'm not saying for a second that you should start writing love-letters to yourself, but I am saying that it's time to give yourself a break. You'd never treat your friends or family like that, so why the hell would you ever do that to yourself?

When somebody comes to me and tells me that they're struggling with self-esteem, the first thing I ask them is:

'Why?' This usually comes as a surprise to them. They're so used to talking themselves down that it's become habitual to them, to the extent that they're now actually shocked that the dim view they take of themselves isn't shared by the rest of the world.

When they've recovered they'll usually say something like, 'Oh, it's because I know other people don't think I'm good enough.'

I said to one lad who gave me this response, 'Who is it who goes around every single day telling you that you're not good enough?'

A pause. A look of confusion on his face: 'Well, no one.'

'Is there a man following you around shouting at you that you're not good enough?'

He smiled at this and chuckled. 'No! Of course not.'

'So why are you so overwhelmingly sure that you're not good enough?'

'You know, my school reports, my exams, that sort of stuff.'

'OK,' I said, 'let's start with your school reports. What are they saying? That you need to work on certain aspects? Make a bit more progress? Or are they telling you that you're a waste of space? That there's no point because you're worthless?'

'They're giving me stuff I need to work on.'

'So they're telling you that you need to improve, not that you're not good enough. There's a bloody big difference.

You just told me that you're not good enough, but you're the *only* person out there saying that. You've convinced yourself that you're not good enough. Those school reports aren't a condemnation, they're a road map showing you where you need to go if you want to improve. They're telling you that *because* they want you to do better, *because* they've got your best interests at heart. And *because* they think you're capable of it. If they'd given up on you, do you think they'd bother? If you can just improve a bit, that's amazing. We all learn in different ways. The important thing, the thing you need to understand is that nobody has ever said to you: "You're rubbish, just pack it in."

'Now let's look at exams. You've had a bad exam result? But that's not who you are. It's just a measure of how you've performed academically on one given day, in one particular subject. It's entirely external, it's noise.

'Let's say that your year at school is divided into different sets for maths. Your friends might all be in the second set, while you're in the third. That doesn't mean anybody is saying that you're not good enough. It's purely an assessment of where your maths is at *right now*. If you'd been put with your friends in set two you probably would struggle and have to go down a set, which really would damage your confidence. What's happened instead is that you've been given a chance to get better, build your confidence, and then maybe at some point in the future take on the challenge of going up a group. The only way is up!'

'It's just what's happened with my son,' I told this lad. 'And what I've explained to you is exactly what I said to him. I don't expect him to change classes immediately. But I do want him to put the work in that means he improves, even if it's just a tiny amount. What he forgets is that while he doesn't find maths as easy as his mate who's in the top set, he thrives at science. He's in the highest group for that because he's fascinated by the amazing world we live in and trying to find out as much as possible about how it all works. He's a victim of the mistake so many of us make – he convinced himself that because he's not good at one thing, then he's shit at everything else.'

FAKE IT TILL YOU MAKE IT?

I'm a bit suspicious of the whole idea that you can 'fake it till you make it'. It feels as if you're trying to build something on fairly shallow foundations. I think a much more secure and enduring way of building your self-belief is actually showing yourself how much you're capable of.

I do, however, absolutely agree that it's a good idea to show the world that you believe in yourself right from the get-go. That sort of confidence is conveyed by the way you look, the way you comport yourself. Is your back straight, can you look others in the eye, do you march into rooms or do you creep into them? You can project confidence, making sure it is the first thing somebody notices about you. For better or worse, other people form their opinions and make their decisions about you on the basis of the version of yourself that you show to the world. So why not make sure that when you meet somebody for the first time, they see the best of you?

EXERCISE
THE CV TRICK

When I talk to people who are struggling with self-doubt and insecurity, there's always one thing I ask them: 'If you were to write me a CV you'd write the hell out of it. I can do this! I can do that! Let's be honest, some of it might be an exaggeration – but of course it is. You really want that job.

   'So why don't you do that to yourself? Why don't you flip that script. If you did get that fictional job, you'd jump in and do everything you can to live up to all the promises you made on your behalf. You'd do it for somebody else. But why won't you do the same for yourself?'

   Stop listening to all of the negative, self-doubting voices that sit inside your head telling you what you can't do. Instead, pretend that you're writing a CV. List all of the things that you can do; commit your positive qualities to paper. This is the person you really are. This is what you're capable of.

LESSONS

- You can build your self-belief by making small commitments. Every time you make a commitment, you're giving yourself tangible proof of what you're capable of. The more commitments you make, the more your self-belief will grow.

- Too often our low self-esteem is the result of the negative way that we talk or think about ourselves. The only reason we think we're a piece of shit is because that's what we tell ourselves all day long. You should look to change the record as soon as you can.

- When somebody tells you that you've got room to improve they're not writing you off, and they're not telling you that you're worthless. They're trying to help you because they believe in you. The correct response isn't to sulk or to let it affect your self-belief – it's to show them that they were right to have faith in you!

CHAPTER 11

YOU'RE STRUGGLING TO COPE WITH LOSS

MY COUSIN GEORGE had a heart as big as the planet. George was a loving, positive kid. He wasn't loud or particularly talkative, but when he walked into a room you were immediately drawn to him. He had that sort of energy.

There was a lovely mischief about him, and an insatiable curiosity. The world was magic to him and he always wanted to know more. Somehow, whenever I went over to his house when I was younger, there would be an alarm raised about George. 'George has gone missing.' I've no idea how many times I heard that. He'd just wander out of the front garden and nobody would know anything of it until a neighbour brought this happy bundle of laughs and jokes back home. They almost always said the same thing: 'Can I keep him?'

His sister has this great story about them after they recently moved to Chelmsford. Their school was a couple of minutes' walk away from their house. One day she was out in the playground when she looked up and saw a nappy-clad toddler bustling past. George! He stopped at the playground gate, calmly waiting for his sister.

But the thing about George was I don't think he ever felt understood, even though he was loved deeply by so many. You could say he suffered right through his life as a result of this. Because he was a wild ball of energy, people saw him as a problem to be fixed rather than as a human being who needed to be listened to and comprehended. He was bright, but the system's sense of what was best for him never co-incided with what he wanted for himself, and what he knew he could achieve.

Quite early on he was diagnosed with ADHD. It wasn't like he had zero concentration or no sense of boundaries, just that he was a hyperactive kid. Make of that what you will. I mean, if they'd been diagnosing that sort of thing back in the eighties then the majority of us might have been given some mild form of that label. I bet I'd have been. I couldn't stop moving, but luckily I had rural France – the whole countryside, with its dens, empty corn fields and endless horizons, was like a huge playground. But London is different. An energetic kid is always going to end up crashing into too many things.

I don't doubt that the people from outside the family who intervened in George's life did so with the best of intentions. And yet it's hard not to wonder whether they did more harm than good. I was talking to my auntie, George's mum, recently, and she'd found some of his old school work – she kept everything of George's; he was her little angel. The book was covered with pictures he'd drawn of his feelings: an angry face, a sad face.

She also showed me a box. George had been seven or eight and came downstairs holding this box, which he'd wrapped up in so much Sellotape it looked like a mummy.

'Whatever you do, Mum, don't open this box until I get back from school. I'm giving it to you to look after, but please, please, please don't open it.'

As soon as he came back that day, my aunt could tell he was happy: 'George, you seem to have had a really good time at school.'

'Yeah, Mum. That's because of the box.'

'Well, what's in the box?'

'I woke up this morning feeling a bit angry, so I put all my emotions into the box and wrapped them up. I wanted to have a good day at school, and I knew that if my emotions escaped everything would be ruined. We can open them up now, though.'

Wow. It blows my mind that he was so young and yet felt as if he had to lock his emotions away like this just so he could get through the day. He'd been told that his emotions were unacceptable; this was his response – a kind of emotional amputation.

George was on Ritalin from a really early age, a drug that zoned him out. And as time went on, the system continued to try to suppress him by categorising him. By its standards, his behaviour wasn't acceptable. From an early age he was bombarded with the same messages we all are: you need to do this, you need to do that. But that wasn't for him, as he had the sort of free spirit that wasn't compatible with tick boxes and rigid ways of looking at the world. He always felt he was capable of doing so much more than the system ever gave him credit for. People thought they were helping him, but the only solution they ever seemed to provide was to force a drab uniformity on him. They should have been helping him grow, but instead they squeezed and shrank his soul. Chucked him a load of medication. Chucked him counselling sessions that never worked.

And because nobody ever taught him how to manage or control his emotions, he was always seesawing between up and down. When he was on medication he could hold down a job. But when he came off it his brain would be turning over at a million miles an hour, pushing him to do stuff that fell outside the narrow limits of the menial job he'd been forced to take.

A bunch of small problems mounted up. Then, one day, everything became too much. He texted his mum, telling her how much he loved her, but also that he didn't believe he was made for this world. George got himself into such a dark place that he made the decision to take his own life. He was just twenty-four.

* * *

DEATH IS AMONG the few certainties in this world. We're all going to depart into that blackness one day, and before we do we'll all lose people we love dearly. That's life. But knowing this will never reduce the pain we feel. When George took the path that separated us from him for ever, it left our whole family stricken with grief. It was too cruel and too incomprehensible a tragedy for any of us to absorb fully.

So many people want to talk to me about loss. They're haunted by the death of parents, partners or friends. They want to know how they can get over the loss; how they can deal with it; how they can move on. Grief becomes another wall standing between them and their chances of living a good, fulfilled life.

A lot of them feel as if they can't let go. Every time they try to get going again they're stopped in their tracks by grief and guilt. 'How,' I've heard countless people ask me, 'can I enjoy my life knowing that they're not with me anymore?'

Their devastation takes them away from their kids, their partners, their work colleagues; all those people who rely on them. Because, ultimately, loss steals something from us all.

I think one of the reasons they approach me is that it's something that I've dealt with since I was young. From the death of my father, through the many tragedies I experienced in the military, on to my mother's death during the pandemic. In many ways, my existence has been defined by death and loss.

And this has been intensified by Covid, which has left so many people mourning lives that ended far too soon. Whole families have been devastated by a cruel virus that attacks every generation.

The first thing I say is that mourning the loss is important. It's an essential part of recognising that there is one thing they cannot do: they can never bring that person back. As horrible and painful as it is for them to have to accept, they need to acknowledge that their loved one is gone for ever. You can't go back in time and stop them from getting cancer, or catching Covid. It breaks my heart to say this, but it's now too late for us to save George.

But you cannot mourn them for ever. Because you cannot allow the loss of those you cherish from stopping you getting on with the only really important business we have: living.

This, for me, is where visualisation comes in. It's something that really helps me in many aspects of my life, especially when it comes to dealing with complex emotions. If I can visualise loss, then it stops being a frightening, incomprehensible force, and starts being something I can touch and understand. In the process it loses a lot of its power.

When we lose someone we care for it creates a gaping void in our life that acts like a black hole. It feels as if this void sucks all the light – and everything good – into it. That was certainly true of my family for a while after George's death.

A lot of people struggling with loss exist in a strange space where the void in their life is simultaneously the most significant element in their existence – it governs their mood, their energy, their ability even to get out of bed in the morning – yet is also something they'll do anything they can to avoid thinking about.

There are two options in this kind of situation. You can leave the void empty, and although you might spend the rest of your life tiptoeing around it, trying to pretend it isn't there, I guarantee you will end up falling into it sooner rather than later. It will appear when you least expect and you'll struggle to get back up.

Or you can try to fill that void with positivity. You'll never fill it completely – some pain will always be there – but you'll reach a point where you live alongside that void without ever being in danger of tipping over into it.

I believe that this is what that person you cared so deeply about would want. They wouldn't want you to become a victim trapped in the void their departure created. They wouldn't want you to lock yourself away from the world, nor would they want you to lose yourself in misery or put your life on hold.

So celebrate that person and their life. Search your memory for all of those fond moments from your shared past that bring a smile to your face. Look at photos of holidays you remember enjoying. Revisit the jokes you shared, or stories of funny things they used to do or say. Talk with others, see what memories they have to share with you. Think about what you're doing now, and who you're doing it for. Celebrate what they brought to your life and to the lives of many, many others. The fact that we are here at all, for any amount of time, is incredible. Our existence is an extraordinary gift that we're given against the odds. The fact that your father died is sad, but the fact that he ever walked the planet, and smiled and cared for you and others is beyond special.

You're not doing this to forget them or to erase them from history. You're doing this to ensure that their legacy lives on. A negative has been flipped into a positive.

My family has done that with George – thinking about all of his jokes and quirks. And I do the same with comrades from the SBS when we get together to reminisce. We sit up until three or four in the morning, chatting about old times, who we were then, what we did.

We'll also talk about the guys who aren't with us anymore. And when we do, we don't think about the fact that they were shot in the head, we laugh at their eccentricities. For instance, there was one lad that loved juggling so much he used to bring all his equipment on tour. You'd come back wired from a mission and he'd be buzzing around our base on his unicycle like an absolute lunatic. That's the image of him that we make sure we all carry around with us.

The process might take months. It might take years. It doesn't matter. Treat it like a lifelong mission. What's important is that when your mind sends you tumbling back into that void your friend or loved one left, you'll find it's filled with positive, happy memories.

When you talk about that person you'll instantly start thinking of all the good things that they represented. So, although that void will always be there, you'll eventually be able to build a bridge across it that enables you to take steps towards a new future that isn't defined by your grief.

Ashley Cain is an amazing example of this. He and his former partner Safiyya Vorajee lost their daughter Azaylia to acute myeloid leukaemia when she was just eight months old. He's dealing with that tragedy in exactly the way I hope I would if, God forbid, anything were ever to happen to any of my kids.

In the spring of 2022 he set out on a 100-mile ultramarathon from Nuneaton to Trafalgar Square in London in her memory. He pushed his body to its absolute limits. Never in a million years would he have achieved something like that if it had not been for what he'd been through. He was dealing with his grief in a way he could understand, doing everything he could to fill the void Azaylia had left with positivity.

The searing pain he experienced during that run helped him understand what his daughter went through. But the pain that was helping him maintain that connection with his daughter was also the thing that was keeping him going. It did not just help him to cope, it allowed him to move on.

I joined him on the final leg to give him some support. I wanted to pump his lion's heart with a bit of motivation. I remember we spoke as he trudged forward.

'Did you ever think you'd do this?' I asked him.

'No. Never.'

'You're doing this because of her. Do you know who gave you that purpose and drive? Your daughter. This is process for progress.'

'Yes.' He picked up his pace.

'Every step you take is another positive memory that will help fill up the void that your daughter left. Azaylia could have just ended up as a statistic. Instead, listen to what people are saying about her. Think about how many orange hearts and balloons you've seen today. That will always be the first thing I'll remember when I think about your daughter. And you've helped do this. You've passed that positivity to so many other people. Look at them – they're smiling, cheering! At the moment, you're living your life through your daughter. But you still have your own life to live. None of what's happened should stop you from going out for a beer with the lads or having nice things.'

He nodded, smiling through gritted teeth.

'How much courage and strength has it taken for you to be out here right now?' I asked him.

'All of it.'

'How easy would it be for you to just go down that little alley there and fall down onto your face and cry? To just quit?'

'I could do that right now, Ant.'

'But you're not going to, are you? Life is one big fight. Now, your fight has just got a bit harder. But you're not going to give in. If anything, what's happened has infused you with even more purpose and passion.'

He carried on. A few hours later he had finished. But I'm still in awe of him and what he achieved.

ONE LAST THING. I know this method works for me, because I've seen what happens when you try to ignore your grief. For twenty-odd years I left empty the void that my father's death had created. Time and again – whether by drinking too much or fighting – I fell into it because I couldn't really accept what had happened, and because I tried to do anything I could to avoid confronting those hard truths.

And then one day I said to myself, 'This has to stop.' I realised that my father wouldn't have wanted me to live in this poisonous cycle of patiently rebuilding everything only to fuck up once more and bring it all crashing down around me. What he would have wanted was for me to be happy, to succeed, to have a lovely family.

So I started to talk about him more. I shared memories with my own family. I celebrated the positive mindset I'd inherited from him, and did what I could to pass that on to my own children. Grain by grain these small, positive actions helped fill the void.

IGNORANCE IS BLISS

George decided he needed to escape from his life. Only he knows why. That's something we always have to accept. George thought there was only one way to deal with his problems, and he did it that way. Now, me and his mum might not have agreed with him, and what he did left us with devastating pain. But it was his decision. Speculation about his reasons won't get us anywhere.

The same is true in the aftermath of any loved one's death. You can't dig yourself into a hole like I did after my father died by asking impossible questions. Why isn't he here? Why don't I have a dad anymore? Why is there nobody to be proud of me? Why is there nobody to be disappointed in me?

That person takes all those answers with them. It might seem hard, and it will inevitably be frustrating, but you must make your peace with everything you don't know, because there's nothing you can ever uncover that will ever make you feel better. There's no question you can ever ask that will elicit a reply that will satisfy you.

EVERYBODY HURTS

You must also remember that you're not the only individual in your circle affected by grief. Think about the impact your behaviour is having on others. Ask yourself again: is this what the person you have just lost would have wanted?

Always think hard about what the grief-stricken need from you. I try never to sugarcoat stuff or to fall back on those awful, useless clichés such as 'I don't know what to say.' What use is *that*? What good do you think that does for them? If you haven't even bothered to think about what those who've lost someone might want or need to hear, then why are you even in this room?

That's the strength that you can bring to the table. If your friend has just lost her dad, you might have been affected, but you're not going through the same grief. So you can bring them an outside perspective, a clarity of mind, that they might find useful, and which for the moment – quite understandably given they're bloodied by pain – is beyond their reach. You can take some of that pain from them.

SLOW AND STEADY

There probably won't be a magic bullet. Whatever progress in dealing with your loss you make will be incremental. It's enough that you feel 0.01 per cent better today than you did yesterday. That's still progress. Yeah, it's going to be shit. It's going to be hard. That's life.

But it will get better if you do this. It *might* get better if you keep hoping for big leaps forward, but you can't rely on it. Swinging from one extreme to the other like George is no way to exist.

So be disciplined. Get into a routine. Leave the house. Being out and about can be a lifesaver. That could be anything from walking the dog to a full-blown workout. On those days when you feel as if there's no hope, seek out the people who love and know you. Use them. Don't feel shy about demanding help. If they've got your best interests at heart they'll give you what you need.

LESSONS

- Grief following a loss will create a terrible void inside you. You cannot ignore it. And you will never be able to rid yourself of it. But you can begin to fill it with happy, positive memories of that person. You'll be ensuring that every time you think of them you'll be celebrating the fact that they existed.

- You should never feel as if you're betraying the memory of that loved one by moving on and enjoying your life. They wouldn't have wanted you to be in mourning for ever; they would have wanted you to be happy. The best way you can honour their memory is to respect those wishes.

- Be like Ashley Cain. Turn your pain into passion. Use all of that grief and emotion to help you achieve something positive, something that you wouldn't have been able to do without this wave of motivation.

- The dead take their truths into the grave with them, so don't drive yourself crazy by asking why they left you or if there was anything you could have done to prevent their passing. If you're never going to be able to find the answer, why hurt yourself by asking the question?

CHAPTER 12

YOU'RE TELLING THE WRONG STORY ABOUT YOUR LIFE

THE STATE OF your life is a reflection of your state of mind. If you live a nightmare in your head, you'll live a nightmare in the world outside your head. And the surest way to create that nightmare is to tell the wrong story about your life.

In jail everyone had their own story. They all gave their reasons for what happened to them, and why. A lot of the men inside faced up to the consequences of their actions. They knew that it was them, and only them, who were responsible for the fact that they'd lost their freedom, and they were determined not to make the same mistakes again.

There was another kind of man there too.

I was part of a veteran community that helped men who'd been in the military with their reading and writing. We'd meet once a week in a nondescript room in one corner of the prison.

At the beginning of each session we'd sit in a circle on uncomfortable plastic chairs and have a brief chat. Some of this was just conversations about their progress. But all of us – helpers as well as those being helped – would also talk about how our lives were going, checking in on each other to see how we all were. Very often the conversation would circle back to our experiences in combat, and the impact on us and our well-being of the things we'd seen and done. We'd talk about our violence and aggression and the importance of cutting both those things out of our lives.

There was one guy, Gary, who was a bit out of kilter with the rest of us. Whereas everyone else was looking to move forwards in some way, he seemed determined to stay exactly where he was.

'My PTSD keeps kicking in,' Gary told us. 'No matter where I'm at, or what I'm doing, it's always there. I'm not in control of my life, my fucking PTSD is.'

A sympathetic silence followed his statement. We all had comrades who'd been altered for ever by the fighting in Afghanistan and Iraq. I spoke up and asked Gary what the trigger was for his PTSD, and where it originated.

'Macedonia,' he said, confidently, as if that explained everything. I think he believed that this would be enough for me. What he didn't know, of course, is that I'd been there too. While I tried to remember what I could of that deployment, he spoke again.

'Yeah, Task Force Harvest, Macedonia, 2001.'

'Oh, right,' I said. I was struggling to think of anything at all that might have happened out there to leave him that traumatised over a decade later. It was a peace-keeping operation in a country that appeared to be on the brink of civil war. The army held checkpoints in rural areas, organised locations for rebels to hand their weapons in and conducted patrols to discourage anybody who might have been thinking about starting a firefight.

'What happened out there?' I asked Gary.

'Just seeing the carnage. The explosions.'

'Right.' I paused. 'But what specific thing triggered you?'

'Well –' he started to reply, now with a note of wariness in his voice. He was on his guard. 'There wasn't one specific thing, but, er, I've not been the same since I came back.'

It was time to show my hand. 'I was out there too. For the whole six months.'

There was complete silence in the room, yet you could feel a crackle of something almost like excitement. Everyone sitting in this circle was aware that the conversation was veering off into a very different direction.

'There weren't any explosions out there,' I continued. 'I worked with the French Foreign Legion, who were responsible for all the mine-clearing. None of them lost their lives. There was one Brit who died; he was in my squadron as it happens. Sapper Ian Collins. He was driving when a couple of kids threw some rocks off a bridge through his windscreen.'

All of Gary's assurance was gone now. 'Yeah, yeah,' he started to say, before tailing off into silence.

'So it was the whole experience of seeing war?' I asked. I didn't want to show him up any more than I already had, even though I knew that his 'experience of war' was limited to the sight of barren streets and sullen rebels handing over antiquated weapons to bored British troops. He probably spent most of his time in a camp doing nothing. Depressing, yes. Traumatic, no.

I addressed the others: 'Was anybody else in Macedonia at the same time?'

The rest of the room shook their heads, as I expected. They were veterans from a different generation. Gary had found his excuse, his get-out card. He was as far from having PTSD as my dog was. There'd been no trauma in his life, and yet here he was claiming that his mental health was the cause of all his problems. He didn't want to take responsibility for his life or the shitty turn it had taken, so he had conjured up a phantom he could blame instead. He wanted to be surrounded by vulnerable people. He was there for the belonging that the group gave him, and I'm not sure he was even that interested in improving his reading and writing. It wouldn't have surprised me if I'd discovered that he was in fact perfectly literate.

At the end of the session I waited until everybody else had filed out of the room before I pulled Gary to one side. 'You need to start being honest with yourself,' I said. 'I was out in Macedonia, I know exactly the sort of tour it was. You need to go away and start being truthful, because all these lies are holding you back. You've got a lot of soul-searching to do, but once you change you'll be freed. It will be as if a weight has been lifted from your shoulders. But right now, you're walking blindly down a road that's leading nowhere.'

His mouth moved a couple of times, as if he were trying to shape some words, but no sound emerged. He knew he'd been caught in a lie. I didn't see much of him after that, so I don't have a neat end to this story.

What I do know is that if he'd carried on pretending that he had PTSD, at some point he'd have actually started to believe he was afflicted by it. And what you believe you become. You – and you alone – will have erected a wall that stops you from ever becoming the real you. You'll die not knowing who you are or what you're capable of. Your potential will all be wasted, your capacity for self-development thrown away. You're going to end up a very fucking lonely person.

GARY IS TYPICAL of all of the most unhappy people I know. They're unwilling to tell the truth about themselves. Instead of accepting responsibility for the twists and turns their lives have taken, they're shot through with bitterness. Because it's easier for them to blame others. It means they don't have to ask themselves any uncomfortable questions or try to work out why they seem to make the same mistake over and over again. It's not that I don't feel sympathy, but fuck, it must absolutely suck to be them.

THE TWO STORIES

There are two stories you can tell about your life.

There's the one with the negative script. In this version of your story you're always playing the role of victim. People who see themselves as victims don't feel any sense of control over the world. This helps them explain away the things that make them uncomfortable. But people who don't feel responsibility for their lives are people who live in a prison of their own making. They're both inmate and jailor. Your focus will be on how much you've suffered, how unlucky you've been and how many people have wronged you. Nothing is ever your fault. Your thoughts are full of phrases like 'I'm owed' or 'I'm entitled to'.

Gary had a negative script for his life. That's why he was always fishing for excuses and telling himself that everyone else had it easier than him.

But you can tell a more positive story too. In this telling, you're responsible for everything you do. You know that although you can't change the cards life has dealt you, you can choose how you play them. Everything is up to you.

Which of these stories do you want to tell about your life? What reality do you want to live in? Positivity is the hardest thing to work on, but it's the most rewarding thing there is once you've figured it out. You'll trip up sometimes. Occasionally you might slip back into your old ways of thinking. But if you're determined, you'll succeed. And after you've done so, your next job is maintaining that positivity – which is where surrounding yourself as much as you can with positive people comes in.

THE 'I CAN'T' FALLACY

Lots of us tell stories about ourselves that aren't true. We say, 'Oh, I'm not the sort of person who can do that.' Or, 'Oh, I'm just naturally very good at this.' It's very hard for us to shake these convictions.

And these stories hold us back. They become self-fulfilling prophecies. If you're always telling yourself that you're no good at sticking to exercise plans, then what chance do you have of ever getting fit? If the story you tell yourself is that somehow you always sabotage relationships, why are you surprised that you're always 'unlucky' in love?

But there's nothing fixed about who we are or what we like. We all have an amazing capacity to grow and learn. So don't put limits on yourself by filling your head with negative myths. Instead of saying 'I can't' all the time, why not try to say 'I can'?

THE ANT FARM

If you zoomed up high above the world and looked down you'd see an ant farm. There are days when I get petrified by the idea that I might be part of it. I know that there's always going to be a system, but I want to be as free from it as I can be. Others, by contrast, are petrified to leave the ant farm, because they believe it gives them security. And, of course, there are those others that don't even realise that the ant farm exists.

Of course, we all have those moments. It happens to me when I'm stuck in a traffic jam on the A12 and I imagine somebody looking down on us. 'How irrelevant am I? What difference do I make? If I disappeared right now, would anybody care?' These thoughts can make me shiver.

At such times we lose our sense of wonder, of the unique connections we can form and the unique impact we have on others. We start saying things like, 'I'm nobody. If I wasn't here on this planet nobody would care – it wouldn't make any difference.' But that is wrong. Oh my God, so wrong. We all serve a purpose. Nobody is nobody. Everyone is someone.

You don't need to be Gandhi or Winston Churchill. You're someone to your wife, you're someone to your kids, you're someone to your friends. In fact, to the people who love you and rely on you, you're *more* important than *anybody* else.

So don't devalue yourself. I fucking hate the nonsense about us just being these specks on the planet who are here for a visit. It makes us sound like ants. It trivialises our lives and makes everything we think, say or do seem insignificant. And I hate the cliché about us being birds sitting on the branches of a tree almost as much. We're not visitors to that tree. We're part of it! We participate in life on earth, we're not just spectators. What do you think happens after we die? Our bodies don't vanish into outer space!

I always urge people to think how awed we all are by the sight of a robot walking unsteadily across a flat surface. Think of all the technology and software that's needed to do just that! It's amazing, but it's nothing compared with what's taking place in our bodies every second of the day. If only people appreciated what an incredible bit of kit they're walking around in. We're all amazing, complex creatures who all have so much to give, if only we would allow ourselves the chance. But, more than that, wherever your thoughts might lead you, you should never forget how much your existence means to so many people. What you do matters. You can make a difference. You *should* make a difference.

THE PAST ISN'T DESTINY

A lot of people use their past as an excuse. I'm not talking about that small but tragic percentage of people who've suffered grievous trauma. I'm talking about the routine damage we all suffer. Those who see their past as a crutch blame it for their insecurities and failures. It explains their lack of motivation and discipline, their struggles with self-belief and self-awareness.

Everything that's behind them ends up as bricks in the wall that stands between them and the best version of themselves. What we all must understand is that the past has happened. Whether it was good or bad, you can't alter it. That's one of the eternal facts of existence. What you can change is how you view it. And once you realise this, it can become an amazingly powerful tool.

When I look back at my life now I see all of the good and bad things that have happened to me. Going to prison was a terrible failure, but it was also the catalyst for the changes that set me on the path to where I am now. The death of my father devastated me, but I also realise that it was in response to his loss that I started to build the resilience that has been so important in helping me survive everything that life has thrown at me in the years since. In fact, I now reckon that that tragedy gave me an early advantage over everybody else. It forced me to self-reflect, to break down my emotions.

I don't see those things as wounds or scars, they're just events or moments in time that have helped create the man I am today.

When you acknowledge this, you're liberating yourself from your past and making sure that you can mould your future. Do you want to be a hero or a victim? That's your choice. Make it. Do you, a grown man or woman, want to be defined by things that happened to you decades ago? It might have been a terrible experience, but you've survived it. Thousands of days, millions of events, have gone by and you're still standing. You must be doing something right. You've still got that will to live. The positive in you must, therefore, outweigh the negative. So why are you letting that one thing determine who you are and what you get out of life?

You must be honest with yourself. You must take responsibility. And I know that's the harder route. It's far easier to blame whatever is happening now on something that's out of your control instead of doing the work on yourself that's needed. You can tell yourself that it's not your fault. So, if that's what you want to do, then fine. Welcome to life on autopilot! But there is another way.

Be honest. Take charge of yourself. Do the mourning or soul-searching or whatever it is that you need to do. More often than not, you'll need to go through a process in order to progress. Don't try to rush it. But never forget that this effort will be repaid a thousand times over.

EXERCISE
FLIP THAT FEELING

The impact of what other people say to you is often determined by your own reaction to it. And I bet you've got a greater capacity to control this than you think.

You can even turn negative encounters with other people into positive experiences. If somebody you interact with says something that upsets you, you could either plunge deep into the victim mentality and dwell on how cruel they were, and how unfair your life is. Or you could see it as a chance to learn a bit more about yourself. Why do you think you reacted so badly? What is it about what they said that triggered you?

By approaching the situation positively you're already robbing it of its ability to upset you. Instead of getting red and screaming, you're just calmly analysing yourself. You're also learning something new about yourself that will help prevent you getting worked up about similar things in the future. Like so many things, you might need to try this a few times before it starts to work for you, but it's 100 per cent worth giving a go.

LESSONS

- Everybody has the ability to act as the author of their own story – it's up to you to use it.

- Your past is not your destiny. Start to live for the person you are now, not for the person you used to be.

- When you tell a positive story about your past, you're helping ensure that you'll have a positive future. If you tell a negative story about everything you've been through, then you're condemning yourself to a negative future.

- When you're lying to yourself, you're living a lie. And unless you can start seeing your personality and behaviour truthfully, you'll go on living that lie until one day you'll wake with a start and realise how much time you've wasted. But by that time it will probably be too late.

- The idea that we're somehow insignificant or that we lead meaningless lives is the fucking ultimate fallacy. You are important to so many people. You make a difference. Never, ever let anybody convince you otherwise.

CHAPTER 13

YOU'RE TOO FOCUSED ON THE DESTINATION

I'VE NEVER SEEN anybody as determined or headstrong as Melissa Wu, the Olympic diver I encountered on the most recent series of *SAS Australia*.

When I first meet somebody, I avoid making any deep judgements about them, but I do try to have a go at making a back-of-the-envelope assessment of their strengths and weaknesses. At first glance with Melissa, I thought that she'd probably struggle with weight on her back – she was five foot nothing.

But then when she actually started in on the course her militant discipline and focus came to the fore. You could see immediately that the deep internal reserves of determination she'd been born with had been sharpened and intensified by the relentless focus – the hours of training, repeating the same action over and over again – demanded by her sport. It sometimes seemed as if she had a nuclear reactor inside her, driving her on.

That mindset set her apart from the rest. She burned with a passion to succeed that none of the other contestants possessed. She committed fully to every task. Nothing fazed her. Then we came to the gas exercise, where the recruits had to go into a Portakabin that had been filled with CS gas. They were told that there was a hostage in there that had to be rescued at all costs. That hostage was carrying a valuable piece of information – it might have been a SIM card, a USB drive or something they'd swallowed – that could help prevent a disaster. I put her respirator on, then directed her towards the building. The idea was that the contestant goes in and gets stopped by the instructor who's already in there. The contestant then gets the chance to assess the situation. They can see the hostage chained up in one corner, and in the opposite corner there's a table with a toolbox. They get three seconds to work out what they need to do, then the instructor takes the recruit's respirator off and pushes them into the middle of the room.

When it came to her turn, Melissa strode in, headed straight for the hostage and started fumbling with the chains, fruitlessly trying to undo them, like they were a knotted rope. Once she began to really cough and splutter, the instructor hurried her out into the fresh air, closing the door after her.

I never grab contestants immediately after a task like this as I always want to give them a couple of seconds to compose themselves. So I waited close by as she stumbled out. Watching her, I thought she'd probably fall to her knees and then cough up all the shit she'd been breathing in.

Instead, she passed out and slammed face-first into the ground. I turned her over, picked her up and realised she was completely out of it. Her jaw had started to lock and I was having to pull out the mud that had rushed into her mouth when she'd hit the deck.

I knew instantly what had happened. A tiny percentage of people have a really unpleasant reaction to CS gas. But that didn't make it any less scary. When she breathed its particles in, it had closed her airway. I put her down on her back and carried on clearing the mud so that she could breathe freely.

Flash. Her eyes opened and she sat bolt upright. She was completely shocked: 'What happened?' What the cameras didn't show were her desperate attempts to return. 'I've got to go again.'

There was only one answer to that: No, you *really* don't. But I seriously think that if I hadn't stopped her, she would have tried. She was still asking to go back even as the doctors were giving her oxygen.

What we couldn't prevent her from doing was returning – still trailed by medical staff – to where the rest of the recruits had gathered. Her mentality was such that, if anything, what had happened had left her even more determined. We decided that the best thing to do was to let her continue, while keeping a discreet eye on her well-being.

The next day involved a boat task. The recruits were assembled on the parade square, where they found two large RIBs (reinforced inflatable boats) filled with ice. We got them to carry the boats around the parade square as hoses were fired into their faces. After we'd been soaking them for about half an hour, I got them to empty the ice out of the boats, and split them into two teams of three. 'Right, lift it above your heads! Until you can hold it still, you're going to have to carry on.'

You could see the boats jumbling about above their heads as they struggled to keep them stable. In an ideal situation, the strongest person would be at the front of the boat, with the two weaker ones at the back. But this hadn't happened in Melissa's group. There were two people at the front of her boat and she, poor thing, was by herself at the back.

All of a sudden the boat dropped on her. Thank God she's a supple, flexible athlete. It send her sprawling to the ground, legs akimbo, head smashing into the dust.

I leapt over to grab the boat and drag her away. When I saw her holding her back I instantly feared the worst.

'Are you OK?' I asked her.

'Yes, staff,' she shot back in a voice that was hoarse with pain.

Getting her to pick the boat up again wasn't an option, but because I wanted to see how she was, I sent the group on a run around the parade square before ordering them to submerge themselves in the trough at its end. I could see that she was still holding her back.

I asked her again, 'Are you OK?'

'Yes, staff.'

I knew she wasn't. But I couldn't force her to admit how much discomfort she was in, even though it was obvious to everyone, even though any other recruit would very likely have quit after the tear gas incident and would certainly have handed their armband in after the boat. I needed her to VW. I *wanted* her to VW. I'd never been in a similar position at any point in any of the hundreds of episodes I'd been involved in. And yet I knew that there was nothing that could make her stop. I knew how much getting through this course meant to her. I also knew that there was nothing here that would justify her sustaining serious and potentially permanent injury. Or even worse.

Of course, next morning, there she was on the parade square. When I asked them if they were ready to go, her 'Yes, staff' seemed to me louder and stronger than anybody else's. 'Here we fucking go,' I thought, any hopes I'd had of her changing her mind overnight well and truly dashed by this tiny Australian Terminator.

Some things are worth suffering for. A TV show really bloody isn't. A moment will always come when you realise that enough is enough. You've already extracted everything you need out of that experience. Whatever's left in it simply isn't worth whatever pain or effort is needed to secure it. That time had arrived for Melissa, but she was so focused on getting to the end that she either didn't notice or had forced that thought out of her head.

That's why, in the end, I had to make the decision for her. She had powered on – God knows how – to the penultimate day. She'd already reached the stage where, as far as I was concerned, it didn't matter whether she actually passed or not. Just getting there demonstrated how phenomenally strong she was in both body and mind. Melissa had nothing left to prove. Nothing.

Her last task in the show was a 3-kilometre run through a mangrove swamp attached by a rope to the four other remaining recruits. The premise was that they were carrying mission-sensitive equipment that was more important than any individual member of the team. The contestants were all clicked onto the rope at 1-metre intervals. If at any point any of them started slowing down the others, then it was either up to them to cut themselves away or for their team-mates to make the decision for them. But I wanted them all to recognise when they had become a burden, to be able to overcome their pride for the sake of the mission.

It was unforgiving terrain. The waterlogged areas were a slog to wade through; they sucked at your feet and every splashy step was an energy-sapping ordeal. The dry areas were even more of a threat. They were all covered in sharp outgrowths of mangrove that stuck up into the air like forks. Anybody unlucky enough to trip up and fall onto them would be in a world of pain.

I started off by really pushing the remaining recruits. It didn't take long for Melissa to stumble. For a couple of seconds she was dragged along by the others, before she was able to scramble to her feet and carry on. As we entered the deepest part of the swamp, she hit the deck again but missed being bayonetted by the vicious mangrove spikes. 'Right,' I thought to myself, 'this is her second lucky escape. I can't bank on her getting the same roll of the dice next time.'

We were twenty minutes in now, with at least another twenty-five minutes to go of battling through brutal terrain, and she was a stumbling mass of pain and exhaustion. It was her determination alone that was keeping her going. She fell again, and, although she got back to her feet, she was clearly being dragged by the others. She wasn't in a headspace to see it, but she was now a burden to the rest of her team and a danger to herself.

What they never showed on the television was that I was running right next to her. I was just saying to myself again and again, 'She's going to go. She's going to go.' I had horrible visions of a mangrove stump spearing into her eye. I could see she was close to passing out. As carefully as I could, I unclipped her and pushed her off to one side. 'You've been amazing,' I told her, 'but you're done.'

WHATEVER YOU'RE DOING, you need to know that you're getting something valuable and progressive from it. If all you're getting out of the experience is pride, then that's not a good enough reason to be throwing your energy into it.

If what you're doing is hurting you and you don't stand to gain anything tangible from it other than being able to say you've 'won', then ask yourself: is this worth it? It's important to know when to move on. Sometimes enough is enough, and it's better to cut your losses and shift your energy in another direction. Pride isn't a good enough reason for pain.

Bonnie Anderson understood that. She knew that she'd gained so much already that she didn't need to go a single step further. She understood that the journey is always, always so much more important than the destination. In fact, she understood one of the most important lessons there is: the destination is irrelevant.

BE A HERO, NOT A MARTYR

For Melissa, failure simply wasn't an option. I suspect she would rather have been carried out bleeding to death than admit that her race was run. In some ways that's an admirable perspective. But in others it's dangerous and futile. There's a time and a place for that attitude: the battle-field.

There are times when 'success' can be more damaging than 'failure'. I stand for ambition and dedication and pushing yourself as far as you can possibly go. But I don't believe in victory at all costs. Be a hero, not a martyr.

Occasionally, you need to count your lucky stars and remember that your limitations are there to protect you from yourself. When people think of Melissa on that show, they don't remember the way she came unclipped from the rope; they think of the ferocious resilience that enabled her to push on after suffering accidents that would have stopped almost anyone else in their tracks. But if she'd stayed on that rope and suffered a nasty injury, or caused the others to fail their task, then that's the image that would have lingered in viewers' minds. That's what she'd take away from it too. Being in control of your own story means knowing when to bring a particular chapter to an end.

If you push yourself until you break, then you're more likely to come away from an experience believing that you're weaker than if you'd let go when you understood the time was right. A moment's pride or stubbornness can end up undoing a lifetime's good work. You will have given your story a nasty twist it doesn't deserve.

A WASTE OF TIME

It's dangerous to be fixated on the destination at the expense of the journey, to place too much emphasis on a 'successful' outcome.

What if you fail? The world is a strange and unpredictable place. Our best plans get derailed by events that smash into us when we're least expecting them. Hard work isn't always rewarded. We can't control how others will respond to what we do.

Let's say your goal is to achieve promotion but despite all your best efforts – putting in extra hours, going on training courses, volunteering to take on extra responsibilities – your boss overlooks you. If you've lived the last six months thinking only about that magic day when you're promoted to assistant manager, then this will come as a crushing blow. You'll feel empty and angry, as if you've wasted time and effort. It will strangle your motivation because you've lost your self-belief. Whatever positivity you once had will have ebbed away, to be replaced by one uncomfortable question: what's the point?

What someone like that won't be able to see is that over the course of those six months they've learned new skills and they've pushed themselves to do things they wouldn't have previously considered. Whatever they do next, they're in a far stronger position than they were when they started out.

But there's something more important too.

THE CITY OVER THE HILL

Too many of us spend our days waiting desperately for the future to come. We tell ourselves that we'll be happy when we finally get that pay rise or that finding a partner will solve all the problems we currently have. Everything will then be brilliant, we say, and until that time we make our peace with the idea of just existing. It's as if we're currently in a waiting room in which we have to sit patiently until our 'real life' starts.

But now *is* our real life. The days we now pass through are all we have. So why not actually *live* in them? Why not make the most of every single one? Why not treat them as if they were important in their own right, not just rungs on a ladder? Look around you, take in everything you see, enjoy the journey.

If you're that person learning new skills because you want to make the next step up at work, then remember to take pleasure in the sensation of being able to do something you couldn't do before. Celebrate the way in which your confidence is growing. If you're doing stuff that breaks you out of your comfort zone, take a moment to appreciate how extraordinary that this is you, doing *this*, something that months, perhaps even weeks, ago, you didn't realise you could do.

All you've got in life is the journey. You don't know what's going to happen in the future, you can do nothing to change the past. So you shouldn't worry about them. Commit to now. Commit to what's right in front of you this minute. That's all that really exists. It's all that really matters.

LESSONS

- A victory won at all costs is not really a victory at all. Nobody gets a prize for pushing themselves until they break because they're too proud to walk away. The important thing isn't always crossing the finish line, it's getting what you need out of any given experience.

- Make sure that you don't get so focused on the destination that you forget about all the worthwhile lessons and experiences you've gathered along the way.

- You can't afford to spend your life waiting for that bright future that lies just around the corner. You must learn to be present in the moment, to focus on what lies before your eyes right now. Because if you don't, you'll barely be living at all.

CHAPTER 14

YOU STRUGGLE TO MOTIVATE YOURSELF

THERE ISN'T A single person on this planet who hasn't, at one time or another, struggled to motivate themselves. That struggle is the villain behind a billion abandoned exercise regimes, an almost infinite number of business ideas that never quite got off the ground, and more unfinished university degrees than I'd care to count.

Sometimes the reasons behind that lack of motivation are clear – perhaps you're in a job that doesn't challenge you or you're putting off doing your tax return. It's difficult to get excited about unpleasant activities! At other times your lethargy is harder to explain. You're given the chance to do something that really interests you, that you know you *should* be throwing yourself into, yet you keep putting off starting on it or continually find yourself distracted. Either way, I hope that this chapter will help you find the energy needed to get up off your couch and start making steps towards becoming a better you.

FIND YOUR PASSION

If you're struggling for motivation, then perhaps it's because you haven't yet found the subject that really interests you. Find something that fills your mind with excitement, that grabs hold of you and won't let go. When you've found something you're passionate about, then you're far more likely to be willing to put in the work that will help you improve. The more stimulating and enjoyable something is, the happier you'll be to work hard at it. After a while it might not even seem like work. And the more you put in to something, the greater its rewards will be.

You don't need to become the best in the world at that thing. Just work out what success on your own terms might mean. But you do need to be passionate about it, otherwise you're going to really struggle. Successful businesspeople don't get up at 5 a.m. every morning because they feel tepid about what they do. The best tennis players aren't out there on the court practising their serve action until their whole body aches because they've got a passing interest in the sport.

Look for something that consumes you. If you find your job tedious or recognise that it doesn't stretch you, and as a result you're struggling to motivate yourself, then maybe it's time to consider switching things up.

DISCIPLINE MAKES MOTIVATION

All of the above is true, but I also understand that 99 per cent of the time, motivation isn't something that descends upon you from the sky. You might be passionate about something, you might really want to put everything you have into it, but somehow you never seem to get started. You put off starting your training for the marathon you're desperate to complete until next week. You plan to wake up a couple of hours earlier than you usually would because you want to work on the business idea that excites you, but you sleep through your first alarm, then your second, and finally decide that maybe you'll just stay in your nice warm bed. You promise yourself that you'll leap into the day tomorrow, and yet come 7 a.m. you're smashing the snooze button again.

Just as often you're faced with something you find boring or unpleasant but that for one reason or another you have to do. When you were a kid that was probably homework. Now it might be a challenging qualification that you need to obtain if you want to progress in your career.

Whatever the reason, if you're trapped behind that wall, then you have to create your own motivation. If the passion you have feels as if it's dormant but you still want to reach that goal, then you need something else to help you along. There's an easy solution: discipline. If you can be disciplined, then motivation will follow.

That's what I told Chloe, who I spoke to after one of my tour events. She was a young mother, with two kids, a job and a busy life. I liked her immediately. She had such a lovely, infectious energy. But she also seemed pretty anguished about her failure to motivate herself.

'I want to lose weight,' she told me, 'but I never seem to find the time to exercise, and when I do I'm too tired, so I just end up sprawled out on the sofa yet again.'

The thing that really frustrated her, she said, was that she knew she was absolutely sincere about getting fit. The idea of it meant a great deal to her. And yet she couldn't find a way of pairing up her passion with the motivation she needed to realise it. She seemed almost perplexed by the situation. It was like she was adding two and two together and getting five. And that left her feeling angry with herself. Which, in turn, made motivation even harder.

I know from experience that it's possible to get accustomed to doing nothing. You get so used to it that suddenly, doing *anything* feels ludicrously hard. That's where Chloe found herself.

'What time do you take the kids to school?' I asked her.

'Well, we leave the house at eight o'clock. Then I go on to work, then I pick them up and when we get home I go straight into doing dinner. That's the problem. There's not even a big enough opening for a short run, let alone going to the gym.'

'OK,' I said, 'if you're saying, "Well, I'd love to make a go of it, but I haven't got time," then you're giving up in advance. If you want it enough, you'll make the time! You've got to be sufficiently disciplined to pick an hour in your day where you're going to give yourself time to exercise. If you want this as much as you say you do, then maybe you'll have to consider getting up that bit earlier. Get out of bed at six and go for a run. Even half an hour is something. But you have to do it, and you have to do it consistently, not just when you feel like it, or when the weather's nice. Don't give yourself excuses. Set your alarm for quarter to six. Try to do it Monday, Wednesday and Friday for four weeks. That's all I'm asking of you. It doesn't matter if you hate it. Just keep going for four weeks. Twelve sessions. A month of your life. Then let's talk again.'

Three weeks later Chloe called me.

'I wasn't expecting to hear from you so soon!'

'I know! But I feel so different. Every morning I wake up ready to attack the day.'

IT'S ALL ABOUT breaking old cycles and getting into a rhythm. To begin with, just try to implement your new regime for a handful of weeks. Don't look beyond that. People are too quick to commit to impossible goals. They write lists with things like 'I'm going to get up at 6.30 and go for a run every day.' This, it goes without saying, is an absolutely catastrophic way to do things. It's too big and intimidating. It feels impossible, because it *is* impossible.

And, because it's impossible, you fail. And when you fail, your motivation takes a big leap off a cliff.

IF, LIKE CHLOE, you can just carve a small amount of time out of your day, then very soon there will be a physical change. Then a psychological change. And that's followed by motivation. It wasn't just that she'd lost a bit of weight. In truth, she probably wasn't that much fitter than she was at the beginning of the new cycle. If anything, her muscles were probably aching. The rest of her body was probably still screaming 'Fuck off!' at her. But she felt good. Just showing herself that she could keep to that schedule made her feel good about herself. I can do this! She realised that she was capable of more than she'd imagined even a month ago.

CUT DISTRACTIONS OUT

I had a similar sort of conversation with my friend Ed, who's also an author. He'd got a new contract to write about a subject he was really passionate about. This should have been a cause for excitement, but when I caught up with him a few weeks later he seemed really low. He told me that his problem was that every morning he'd wake up full of motivation, rush down to his desk and turn his computer on. But that's where his problems started. He'd look at the expanse of empty white on his screen, and the cursor that seemed to be flashing impatiently at him, and all the hours he had to somehow use productively until 5 p.m., and instantly feel panicked. He'd try to get going, and yet time after time his mind would wander and the next thing he knew he'd been pissing about surfing the web for two hours. Or he'd suddenly decide that it was really important to polish his shoes or pump up his bike tyres or make a big pot of soup. Anything except the thing he was supposed to be doing.

Just like Chloe, he couldn't understand why he found it so hard to match the passion he had for what he did with the motivation he needed to actually do it. He'd reach the end of every day feeling tense and angry and full of self-loathing.

The solution for Ed was similar to the one I suggested for Chloe. Except his problem wasn't that he didn't have enough time. If anything, he had too much of it. In order to build his motivation, he needed to find discipline, and he also needed to work out how to make himself less vulnerable to distraction.

Ed bought a program that allowed him to block the internet. Then he set it to work for twenty-five minutes. After that, he'd give himself a five-minute break, before turning the internet off for another twenty-five minutes. It all sounds really simple, but that small thing completely transformed

THE WALL

his productivity. All he had to focus on was twenty-five minutes of work. Instead of feeling overwhelmed and constantly vulnerable to distraction, he had a disciplined structure. Instead of feeling frustrated and demoralised at his lack of progress, he was full of motivation. When he closed down his laptop in the evening he could look back and feel proud of how much he'd accomplished.

WHEN WE LACK motivation, distractions can really prey on us. And, unfortunately, the modern world is absolutely brilliant at creating things that constantly undermine our ability to focus on what matters most to us. I helped Ed identify what it was that impaired his ability to concentrate, and showed him how to break a big, amorphous task into smaller, more manageable chunks. If you're struggling like Ed, these are strategies you could employ too. You might also want to consider your environment (mess and noise limit our ability to focus) and even giving yourself small rewards (which could be anything from some food to a few minutes on Instagram) as an incentive to be more productive.

The other thing that I know can wreak havoc with your ability to focus on the task before you right this minute is the knowledge that there's other stuff in your life that's demanding your attention at the same time. That could be another job you've left unfinished, or maybe you've argued

240

EXERCISE
THE PLAN

A lot of the people who approach me for tips to help with their motivation are like Chloe. They want to take more physical exercise, but really struggle to find a way of fitting it into their full lives. Somehow, between family, work, socialising and everything else, there's no time to go to the gym, the swimming pool or out on that run. All their best intentions go up in smoke.

I say the same thing to all of them: you need to find a way of integrating physical activity into your routine. I actually plan in advance when I'm going to exercise, and then make sure that I keep a suitable amount of time free. In addition to that, I think about whether I need to go to anywhere special to do it and also whether I need any equipment.

That's all pretty easy. The important thing is that you do the same thing at the same time every week, so that it becomes a habit.

Think about what kind of exercise you'd like to do, then try to answer the questions below.

- What do you want to do?
- When can you do it?
- Where can you do it?
- What do you need to do it?

with your partner and anger or annoyance is eating away at you. It's so important to do everything you can to square away any loose ends that have the potential to unsettle or derail you. That's why I never go away on a work trip distracted. If I've had a falling-out with Emilie, I make sure we've made up properly. If there's a wrangle over a contract, I'll make sure it's fixed. Because I know that there will always be part of my mind that's elsewhere when I want to be 100 per cent focused on my job.

THE TIME IS NOW

You cannot wait until tomorrow, or next week, or next month, or next year. You cannot wait until your head feels right or you're more full of energy or they've stopped digging up the street outside. Postponing things is really just a way of saying you're never going to do it. It's a lie we tell ourselves because we're not quite ready to admit the truth.

You have to make a commitment to start now. It's just one piece of effort, one decision. Nothing more. Just. Fucking. Start.

LESSONS

- The more passionate and interested you are in something, the easier you'll find it to motivate yourself. So if you're struggling for motivation, perhaps it's time for a change of activity. If you hate running, then you're going to find it really tough to summon up the energy and enthusiasm needed for a marathon.

- You can, however, create your own motivation. Discipline is key here. You shouldn't ask too much of yourself, nor should you give yourself excuses. If you've committed to running three times a week, then you've got to run three times a week. If you can just stick at it, the reward will come far sooner than you think.

- Distraction is the enemy of motivation. Try to identify everything that could get in your way or rob you of your focus — whether it's a blinking light in your study or an unresolved problem in your personal life — and neutralise it.

CHAPTER 15

YOU THINK YOU KNOW EVERYTHING ALREADY

YOUR HOME, FOR as long as the mission demands, is an improvised piece of cover. Perhaps an irrigation ditch that you've built up with vegetation and rocks until you're happy that you can work unseen.

You move there when it's dark, to avoid detection. Dawn finds you lying on your front, peering through the telescopic sights of your rifle.

You trace the sun's path as it creeps up over the valley. Slowly, steadily, it becomes easier to see your target. You're there to watch, to wait. Watching comprises maybe 99 per cent of your time. Sometimes you'll need to pull your trigger, but more often than not you won't. Watching is a skill, like any other. And so much of what you do is the result of hours of practice and study. The patient, at times painful, acquisition of that skill. Drill after drill after drill.

I remember the training I received back in Lympstone Commando when I was just a rookie. We were taught that sniping wasn't about the excitement of a kill shot or the glamour of stalking prey. It was about precision, diligence, care. It was about carrying a little notebook – your sniper log – with you wherever you went. If you went out onto the range to practise, you'd record the wind strength, the humidity, the barometric pressure and the air pressure in its pages, then make a note of the adjustments you'd made to your weapon in order to account for it all and get the perfect shot. Watch, record, then the grinding experience of firing round after round after round after round, until you get it.

You then carry out this procedure in all sorts of different conditions and locations. The number of variables you had to process was incredible – you had to know exactly how to breathe; if your target was further than two kilometres distant, you had to account for the rotation of the earth – and every single one had to be understood and accounted for.

It is only then, after the slow, repetitive process of training, that sniping starts to become instinctive. You begin making your own calculations subconsciously. You find yourself just thinking, 'Right, we're 500 metres away, these are the conditions, that means four clicks to the right, two clicks up.'

It is not an appetite for blood that makes a good sniper, but an appetite for knowledge.

You focus on a bazaar on the outer perimeter of a village. It should be bustling with traders, mopeds and donkeys pulling carts. But it's deathly quiet, with almost everything boarded up with corrugated iron. So you watch, you wait.

You home in on the buildings in the village one by one. You draw sketches on a paper and pad, recording any intelligence you can. In the moment, your work seems futile, the obsession with details pointless. But every new piece of information helps build the pattern you need. So you watch, you wait. Who is walking in and out of where? What can you see through the windows? You log the cars coming and going.

There are false starts. Moments that look as if they're going to be meaningful, but end up being irrelevant. You will notice something moving on the roof of a house. Perhaps this is it? A shiver of excitement runs down your spine. 'Movement on the roof of Building 7,' you tell your partner. So you watch, you wait. But the movement stops. At some point you realise that nothing is going to happen.

It's still only 16:00. That means another seventeen hours in the irrigation ditch. That means a long, cold night. But your mission is not over, you cannot afford to miss a single thing. So you watch, you wait.

WHEN YOU'RE ARROGANT, when your mind is closed to new ideas and new concepts, when you think there's nothing left to learn, you're guaranteeing that at some point you're going to have a very fucking uncomfortable collision with that wall.

Because if you stop learning, you'll stop growing. And if you stop growing, you're going to end up stuck. You must be humble. There's no shame in not knowing how to do something. You should never feel embarrassed about asking questions. But you should feel humiliated if you're the sort of person who feels that they need to hide their ignorance behind a wall of bluster and lies. If you pretend you know more than you actually do, you're doing nobody a favour, least of all yourself.

It's important to understand, however, that education isn't just about degrees and certificates. It's also about what you learn from other people, what you learn from experiences. It's about cultivating a mentality that's always alert to what the world can teach you.

Some people have a shit experience at school because it doesn't fit their skills. Academic learning isn't for everyone. I should know, I left school without a single qualification. And some people have a shit experience at school because they're too good at it. Their life gets defined by a suffocating pressure to perform at a high level in an endless series of tests. Both types of person, for different reasons, get put off learning for the rest of their lives.

But the point about education is that if you strip everything else away, it's about becoming a better version of who you are. It's not about pleasing other people or ticking boxes. Learning is something you do for yourself, not anyone else. That's the message I've tried to pass on to my kids. I don't need them to come top of the class. Education isn't a competition. But I do want them to try their hardest and to make incremental improvements, because in doing so they're building a foundation for themselves that will serve them well later in life.

You need to find a way of learning that suits you. That could be formal courses, it could be reading books, it could be YouTube videos, it could be talking to people who can help you get on. That's exactly what we did in the Marines as we learned the craft of sniping. Most of us weren't bookworms. A lot of us hadn't got on very well at school. But the pride we felt when wearing that green beret gave us a motivation to better ourselves in other ways. So we sought out those who we knew were experts at what they did and pumped them with questions about every aspect of their work. We threw ourselves into trial and error, because we knew that by trying and failing until we'd figured a particular problem out, we'd learn so much more than if we'd just picked up a manual. In the process of gathering that knowledge, we made sure that we moulded it into something we could understand. Learning can be as much about what works in practice as what works in theory.

THE FOUR CORNERS

Formal education is great. It's really important to study hard, whether you're at primary school or university. But you should never forget that outside the four corners of the classroom are the four points of the world. If you can combine the four corners and the four points – the eyes in the sky and the boots on the ground – then I guarantee that'll supercharge your learning.

BECOME A WATCHER

I love life. I'm fascinated by it. And I know I'll never lose that fascination. There's so much to learn. I'm forty-one now, and I'm so excited to find out how I'll be thinking when I'm eighty-two.

The fascination I feel is fuelled by the fact that I'm a watcher. I'm curious about everything that goes on around me. It's something I've always been, but I think my time as a sniper made me more systematic about it. Even now, I learn so much from face-to-face interactions. I get a buzz from paying attention to the energy we give off and the ways in which we engage with one another.

When you start watching the world closely, you begin to learn so much more. It's a really valuable lesson in the importance of getting out of your own head. You find that you can learn from your own experiences and become a whole lot better at spotting little things that you can pick up from others – whether it's a particular skill or just a clever way of dealing with a situation.

If you pay close attention to the people around you – be they family or your colleagues – you'll see very clearly what makes them tick, so you'll be better able to anticipate their emotional needs and what sorts of things they respond to. Do they react better to the carrot or the stick? Can you trust that guy in your team to get on with a job without much supervision, or do they need to be micromanaged? What are the particular things that trigger stress in your husband?

Watch. Learn. Repeat.

BE HUMBLE

When I started working in television I knew jack-shit about the art of putting together an hour-long programme. I was actually so green that occasionally I'd feel intimidated by the thought of everything I didn't know. Each day when we went out on set I'd feel baffled by some of the things that the directors were asking us to do. I'd always end up standing in the wrong place, talking to the wrong camera. I was ignorant of the jargon and language. Sometimes a runner would ask me what they thought was a straightforward question, and I'd look at them blankly, as if they were talking to me in Swahili.

I had two options. One was to style it out and pretend that I knew more than I did. I reckon I could have got away with that. The great benefit of walking into a room where everybody knows you're fresh out of the Special Forces is that very few people are willing to call you out, even when you're doing or saying something stupid.

The other route to take was to humble myself, admit I barely knew the basics and ask question after question. After a while I realised how much I enjoyed that feeling of being thrown into the deep end. I like starting right at the bottom, knowing that the only way is up; it's exciting to get a sense of how much you have to learn. But you'll only get the benefit from that if you're willing to admit – not just to yourself but to others around you – that you know enough to know that you don't know enough.

HOW TO DEAL WITH CRITICISM

I think we should all learn to welcome positive criticism, although there's no denying that it can sting when you first hear it. You're only human, so initially your pride will probably be hurt. You might even start to doubt yourself, especially when you have stepped out of your comfort zone to try something new.

When somebody criticises me I do a couple of things. The first is that I remind myself that we all make mistakes some of the time. There's usually something we could be doing better and there's no shame in messing up. The next thing I do is to interrogate what exactly it is I'm feeling. Am I angry with the person who has called me out, or am I actually angry with myself for having dropped a bollock in the first place? I try to work out why it's provoking such emotion in me. Perhaps the criticism is unfair and they're just taking a pop at me. If that's the case then I swat it away. You're never going to learn anything from the sort of sniping, bitter criticism that you get from jealous, resentful people.

But if I see that the person who has corrected me is trying to help me rather than make me look stupid in public, I'll do everything I can to absorb what they have to say. You should always listen when criticism comes from somebody who cares about you, someone who simply doesn't want to see you make the same mistake twice.

Of course, there isn't anybody alive who doesn't like being told how amazing they are. But at the end of the day, praise doesn't teach you anything. How would you ever have learned to drive, or earned a professional qualification, if nobody had ever criticised you?

That's why I'm always puzzled by those people who think they've exposed me as a hypocrite because I'm sometimes harsh on contestants: 'How can you call yourself positive when we've all seen you bawling out ...?'

Yeah, you're not as clever as you think. There's always a positive in what I do. I know that telling that person they're wonderful isn't going to help them realise their potential. But I'm actually extremely protective of the recruits. For the duration of the time they're on the show, they might as well be my children. Woe betide the person behind the camera who accidentally knocks one of them over. I'm just desperate for them to become the best version of themselves that they can be.

What I want is for you to understand the same thing about feedback and criticism as the show's most successful contestants do. It's not somebody pushing you down – that person is giving you a hand up.

LEARN FROM THE BEST

Part of humbling yourself is realising that there are many, many others who know more than you. Instead of trying to compete with them or getting intimidated by what they've achieved, why not listen to them and learn? Seek out the people who are the best in your field. Work out what they do that sets them above everybody else, then see what parts of that you can apply to your own life.

LESSONS

- You're never going to get anywhere worth going if you don't learn the things that are worth knowing. I left school without a single qualification but I know the value of learning. You should make sure that you do too.

- Don't make the mistake of thinking of education as something that only takes place in a classroom. There are so many different ways to acquire knowledge. So find out what works for you.

- Theoretical and practical knowledge both have their advantages. But ideally you'd combine both. If you can combine the four corners of the classroom with the four points of the world, you'll be unstoppable.

- Be humble. Be the sort of person who knows enough to know that they don't know enough. And never feel afraid of admitting your ignorance. It's OK to ask questions, it's not OK to try to blag your way through life.

- Praise is great, but you can't learn from it. So embrace criticism. It's a crucial part of growing and learning. If you ignore it you'll be shutting yourself off from an important element in your personal development.

CHAPTER 16

YOU OVER-THINK SITUATIONS

WHAT I LOVE about mountains is the freedom they represent. Pure and utter freedom. No one can tell me to come down. Not the police, nor the pope, nor the president of the United States. That decision is completely mine. There are no restrictions, no limitations, nothing to suppress or shackle me. All of that just falls away. If I want to climb up to the summit and never descend again, I can. I always return from my journeys up mountains energised and excited. I never come back the same person.

There is nothing and nobody to tell you who you are or who they think you need to be. On the mountain, you and your actions alone define you. You feel bonded to the people you're with. You all have the same objective.

Some people talk on the mountain, just as they might chat to a friend they've bumped into in the supermarket. Everywhere else I'm a talker, a hyperactive blur of conversation and thoughts. But up there I'm almost silent. I say what I need to, and not a single word more. The only thing I want to hear is the regular thud of my heart. I want to take everything in, to appreciate its majestic simplicity. I want to embrace the moment I'm in.

When you're up there in the mountains in the freezing air, surrounded by jagged rocks and vast expanses of glistening white snow, it clears your mind. It might sound strange, but you switch off. The experience can feel so gruelling, so tough, that your world shrinks to a single act: putting one foot in front of the other. You don't think about anything else, because you can't think about anything else. It's the ultimate simplification in life, existence stripped back to its most basic elements, a reminder that the only important thing is what's right in front of you, this minute.

When I'm in the mountains I feel more in tune with the world. It makes me look at life in a different way. There's something so exciting and liberating about knowing that no matter how challenging or dangerous or complex, there will always be a way up. You get addicted to that feeling. I've got a sleeping bag, food, I've got a stove, I'm surrounded by snow that I can melt when I need a drink. What more do I need? The simplicity of it all is mesmeric.

It gives you a new perspective on your life. I feel gratitude when I'm on a mountain. It stops me taking things for granted. You feel your real emotions. You realise how much you miss some people; how much you love them.

And as you're scooping a pile of snow into your pan to melt on your stove, suddenly a solution will present itself to an issue that had seem impossible to resolve. There's no effort. You're solving problems almost without realising that you're doing it. That brings with it peace. It's only by being up there that you realise how plagued by distractions our everyday lives are: phones, doorbells, work anxieties, delivery drivers, guilt, school runs, people who want or expect you to do stuff for them. We're slaves to all these things. You now see how irrelevant that situation is that's been bugging you so much back home. It now becomes clear that all of the stress and pressure that feels inevitable when you're down at sea level is in fact self-induced. You can just drop it.

You realise that the world we live in doesn't make our lives complex.

We do.

I OVER-THINK, THEREFORE I AM

A lot of the complexity we experience in our day-to-day lives comes from that capacity we all have to over-think.

We're in the strange position of being apex predators who used to be a *lot* further down the food chain. Tens of thousands of years ago, to be human was to be permanently aware of a host of dangers. This means that we're evolved to be acutely sensitive to threat, which in turn means that we take in nine times as much negative information about the world as we do positive. Our outlook is inherently anxious.

When you fall into the trap of over-thinking, your brain goes into a negative spiral and it's difficult to get anything in the right perspective. You can't see things clearly. You attach exaggerated levels of importance and meaning to insignificant gestures or words or facial expressions. 'I wish I hadn't said that yesterday. Why did I say that yesterday? What will Sam think of me? I wonder how she interpreted it? Omigod. She probably hates me.'

When I was in the Special Forces, that way of looking at the world could have cost me my life. The first man in doesn't get a chance to over-think. So I had to learn to keep things simple. Break things down. Keep them black and white. The world is full of polar opposites. Once you recognise that, everything becomes much simpler. If things don't work for you, they'll work against you. If you can't be honest with yourself, you'll be living a lie. If something isn't progressive, it'll be regressive.

I don't see the need to make things any more complex than that. Life is complicated. We are very complicated beings. Why *add* any more complexity to the mix? Now, when I get over-involved in an argument, or a particular problem keeps turning over and over in my head until I begin to worry I'm going mad, I try to imagine what I'd think about these things if I were on the upper slopes of a mountain, freezing my bollocks off and wondering how the fuck I'm going to get to the summit.

Almost invariably, the answer is that they're not worth another second of my time or attention. Like I said, keep it simple. Complexity is over-thinking's closest ally, simplicity is its deadliest enemy.

GET THIS BIT DONE RIGHT NOW

Narrowing your focus is often a great way of combatting the temptation to over-think. Don't worry about what's coming down the road, just concentrate on what's in front of you. Don't get bound up in the billion little permutations of what *could* happen – if you do that, you'll be overwhelmed.

When I was on the boat during *Mutiny* I didn't spend much time thinking about the thousands of miles we still had left of our journey, I focused on the twelve miles that were immediately ahead of me. Or when we were on *Escape* salvaging bits of engine, I didn't think too much about the intricate difficulties we might face integrating the engine with other bits of machinery. We just had to get it to work.

You need to focus squarely on what you know is happening right now, not what you worry might happen in some imaginary future. Privilege the stuff you can hear and see, not the stuff you conjure up in your mind.

REMEMBER YOU'RE A PROBLEM-SOLVER

I've talked before about how we're a species of problem-solvers. It's one of the things that distinguishes mankind from the rest of the animal kingdom.

This ability has come to our aid countless times over the course of our time on the planet. It's meant we could work out how to cook meat at one end of history and develop Covid vaccines in record time at the other. And it can come to your aid when you've tumbled deep down an over-thinking rabbit hole.

Instead of torturing yourself by trying to work out all the ways the future could go wrong, why not focus on thinking about what you could do to prevent your worst-case scenarios from happening at all? Or challenge yourself to identify five potential solutions to them in the unlikely event that the doomsday you've spent your life predicting actually does arrive. It's much more helpful to focus on how a problem can be fixed than it is to dwell endlessly on the problem itself. Your brain will be working so hard on trying to come up with constructive responses that might actually make a material difference to what you're going through that it won't have time to get lost in a negative spiral of thoughts that will only make things worse.

CHAOS VS CONTROL

We're not always good at remembering that a very large proportion of what goes on in the world is completely outside our control. Many people get obsessed with trying to exert some kind of power over things that just aren't within their grasp and never will be. It means that they lose sight of the things that they *can* control.

It also leads to over-thinking, because if you start considering all the things that *could* happen, then you're never going to stop. You'll simply end up in a negative spiral, filling your mind with a million doomsday scenarios. What if this happens? What if that happens?

I always say to people who are anxious and stressed, 'Write a list of all the stuff that's bothering you. Then, as soon as you've done that, cross out all the things that you can't control. Don't give them even a second of your thought or energy because doing so is an appalling waste of your time.'

I guarantee that in a ten-strong list of worries, no more than three will be things that you can control. Why focus on that elusive 70 per cent when there's 30 per cent that you can have a real impact on?

Otherwise that 70 per cent that you can do *nothing* about will be swirling around your head, so much so that you lose sight of the 30 per cent you can do *something* about.

So, if you're having problems with your boss, work out which bits of the situation you can control and which you can't. Focus on the stuff that you make a difference to, and let go of the stuff you can't have an impact on.

You can go into the office, ask to see your boss, and tell them that you feel as if you're being treated badly. You can control that, so don't shy away from the decision you *need* to make. You cannot control how they respond, but you can control what you say to them, how you say it. You can control the way you present yourself. You can control the way you react to whatever they might say to you in return.

But there's other stuff you'll never be able to control, and the sooner you can make your peace with it the better. Not for a single moment would I deny the reality of climate change. It's clearly a challenge that as a world we're going to have to address, and sharpish. But it's not something that you, as an individual, can do anything significant about. You might be able to do some recycling, use your bike more and cut down on single-use plastics or whatever. Indeed, you *should* be doing that sort of thing. But there's absolutely no way you can stop massive power stations and factories in China or India belching fumes into the atmosphere. You're never going to be able to get between the Americans and their desire to fill their massive, fuel-guzzling vehicles with petrol or diesel.

So don't get drawn into apocalyptic speculation. Do what you can. Don't worry about what you can't. As soon as you do, you'll get sucked into a negative spiral. When you're anxious about something that's outside your control, your sense of dread will inevitably just grow and grow. And this is precisely *because* you can't do anything. If you're worried about the state of your teeth, then the solution is easy and absolutely in your hands: brush your teeth more regularly, buy some floss, see a dentist! But what are you going to do about the polar icecaps? Seriously! Because you'll start feeling guilty about something that in no conceivable scenario is your responsibility.

This isn't a call for you to cut yourself off from others or to dismiss your feelings of empathy. It's just a realistic appraisal of what we can and can't do. And it's also an acknowledgement of the limits of our mind and bodies. We have enough fucking things to worry about as it is. Why *increase* that burden?

TOO MUCH KNOWLEDGE CAN BE A BURDEN

Just as it's possible to think too much about a subject, it's also possible to know too much before you go into a situation.

Mutiny is a good example. Before I set off on that epic journey around the Pacific, I made a conscious decision *not* to read Captain Bligh's journals. I didn't want to study who he was as a man or what sorts of decisions he took. I knew that if I tried to replicate how he'd succeeded, I'd leave myself in the unfortunate, and painfully ironic, place of guaranteeing my own failure.

That knowledge would have inhibited me. I wouldn't have been able to see clearly. Every time a new challenge or problem presented itself, a little voice in my head would have piped up: what would Bligh have done? Instead of responding to the situation in the moment, actually looking at what was in front of my very eyes, I'd be defaulting to another person's experience and ideas. It would lead to me second-guessing every call I made.

I knew what my job was: I had to sail 4,000 miles in a 23-foot open boat manned by a crew that was subsisting on 350 calories a day. As far as I was concerned, that was where the similarities between Bligh and me started and ended. I didn't get carried away studying which islands he stopped off at or what precise route he took. I certainly didn't want to spend too much time learning about how he motivated his crew (clue: there's a pretty good reason why he was chucked off his boat in the first place; the only surprise to me is that there was only one mutiny!). I knew that I was a good leader. I'd proved that to myself on the battlefield time and time again.

So don't cloud your head with what somebody else might do. As I've said a million times before: you'll never be able to fit 100 per cent into another individual's skin. But you're a perfect fit for your skin. What would *you* do? Don't pass the buck, don't hand over responsibility to another person. Take that responsibility. What would *you* do?

When you overload yourself with too much information about what *other* people have done, it limits you as an individual. And, even more dangerously, that extra knowledge gives you a whole load of unnecessary ammunition that enables you to avoid doing things; the negative part of you is simply desperate for reasons to persuade you to shy away from this decision or that adventure. Your mind fills up with a jumble of 'what ifs?' and worst-case scenarios. It becomes so overwhelming that, especially if you're predisposed to suffer from anxiety and stress, you just stay the hell away. And guess what? Your life gets a little smaller as a result.

EXERCISE
CHALLENGE YOUR NEGATIVE ASSUMPTIONS

When you can feel your negative thoughts begin to spiral inside your head, you can try to reframe the way you think about the situation you're contemplating so that your focus switches from negative to positive outcomes.

The first stage is to work out what it is exactly that's troubling you – you can't tackle a problem properly if you can't see it clearly.

It might be something like: *I'm worried that if I take this job I'll be exposed as a fraud. I think I'll make a mess of it, and that will make me look stupid in front of people whose opinion I value. That will have a knock-on effect on my confidence. If I fail at this, I don't think I'll have the courage to ever try something like this again.*

Then ask yourself how imagining this outcome – failing at the job – makes you feel: *Frankly, I just want to stay in bed and put my head under the covers.*

But what if there was another way of looking at this situation? What if the worst-case scenario stopped being your default assumption? Now try to imagine what it would look like if you took the job and things went well: *I know I'm qualified for the job, and I'm pretty sure I'd really enjoy it. I could end up thriving. And just going for it would make other people respect me.*

How does adopting this positive perspective make you feel? *Motivated. Excited. I'm really keen to just get cracking and put my application in.*

This is a great habit to develop. The more you practise swapping negative outcomes for positive ones, the more likely you are to start doing this automatically.

LISTEN TO YOUR BODY

A lot of the time our over-thinking is fed by nervous energy. Our whole body feels as if it's been flooded with adrenaline, and maybe one leg begins to jog up and down, as if it has a life of its own. And then our anxiety begins a negative spiral. It's your body telling you something! Whenever that happens to me, I find the best thing to do is to divert that nervous energy into a positive direction. Instead of sitting down and letting my mind fill with worries, I'll go to the gym. Afterwards I'll always feel calmer. You can achieve the same by taking the dog for a walk, or getting your skipping rope out for ten minutes, or turning cartwheels. Do whatever helps you to work that nervous energy out of your system.

LESSONS

- We live in a bewilderingly complex world that gets more complicated with every passing day. Over-thinking only adds to the complexity, so why the fuck would you do that to yourself? Your mantra should always be: 'Keep it simple.'

- Try to see the world in black and white. Don't make things any harder than they need to be. Is this thing good for me or bad for me? Yes or no?

- Don't stress yourself out by thinking about the bad thing that might possibly, potentially, maybe happen in six months' time. Work out what you're confronted with RIGHT THIS MINUTE. Then deal with it.

- You must try to control everything in your life that you can control, because there's a hell of a lot out there that you can't control. And when you realise you can't control a situation, let it go. If you can't stop the ice caps from melting, then don't expend energy worrying about them.

- Learning is vitally important. But thinking *too* much can be a burden. Don't let your brain obsess about information it doesn't need to get the job done.

CHAPTER 17

YOU STILL BELIEVE THAT PERFECT IS POSSIBLE

I USED TO believe in perfection. I absolutely do not anymore. I've come to understand that nothing and nobody is perfect. I believe that the sooner you work that out and make peace with it, the sooner you can start living a meaningful, fulfilling life. But the tragedy is that there are still so many people out there who eat themselves up in the pursuit of something that doesn't exist.

It's easy to see why – perfection is such a seductive idea. Surely wanting to be perfect is a good thing? It's pure, it's faultless, it's the result of hard work. We're all taught to admire people who claim to be perfectionists.

And yet there isn't an individual alive who doesn't have flaws. No person in the course of history has ever got through their life without making mistakes. It's just part of what it means to be a human being. Somebody who continues to think that perfection is possible is denying that reality.

I also see now that a belief in perfection is really just another way of not rising to challenges, even another way of lying to yourself. Because if you can convince yourself that the reason you're still sitting on your couch is because you're waiting for perfection, that thing that's always just around the corner, then you can postpone all the important decisions and commitments you need to make.

This is true of those people who are waiting for the 'perfect' opportunity, which really means that they end up stranded. It's true too of the writer who keeps working and working at his novel, refusing to send it out into the world because he's afraid that people won't like it. He knows that this is an excuse. You might think that you're doing the right thing by insisting on perfection. But what you're really doing is building a wall around yourself.

It was failure that made me realise that the idea of perfection is a dangerous illusion. All those fuck-ups freed me. They showed me that you learn a thousand times more, you become a thousand times more resilient, you open yourself up to a thousand times more opportunities, by failing and bouncing back than you ever would in a fruitless quest for perfection.

So, for example, somebody who still believes in perfection will look at a job opportunity and all they'll see are the flaws. Every one of those flaws gives them a reason to postpone committing. Not for ever, they tell themselves, but just until the 'perfect' job opportunity comes up. It's a negative mindset draped in a positive-looking cloak.

But you need to go on that journey, because along the way you're going to pick up those little percentage improvements that will push you closer and closer to becoming the best version of yourself. You'll be able to add new experiences, and new ways of seeing the world and solving problems, to your psychological bank.

Practice doesn't make perfect. It can't make perfect. Nothing can. But practice does make progress.

AMY WAS SO hard on herself. I've got no idea where the pressure to be perfect came from, but it was strangling her.

All her life she'd worked really hard, and anyone watching would think that she'd reaped the rewards that her efforts deserved. She was a high-flying lawyer with a lovely family, living in a beautiful house. They took regular holidays, and she and her husband drove nice cars.

But she couldn't take any pleasure in any of this. Instead of thinking about everything she *had* achieved, she was fixated on what she *hadn't* managed to do. She told me that even twenty years on, she was furious about the fact that she'd only come second in her law class. There were times when she listened to her daughter practising the piano and found herself criticising the couple of tiny mistakes her kid had made instead of praising her for the amazing progress she'd made. She hadn't intended to give her daughter a bad review, it was just her instinctive reaction. Amy knew that her relentless insistence on perfection was damaging her and risked being passed on to her family, but she couldn't see her way out of that mindset.

I explained to Amy that if you always insist on perfection, you're guaranteeing you'll never be happy. If you think that you're a failure if you're not top of the class every time there's a test, you're setting yourself targets that are impossible to reach. Once you can accept that you won't always get things right and that there are things about you that aren't perfect, then life becomes a lot more straightforward.

'You might make a mistake here and there,' I said. 'Occasionally you might fall short of the standards you ask of yourself. But nobody around you will love you any less as a result. You're still the same person as you were before. It doesn't change your value in any way. What I've realised is that I'm still the same person whether I've just knocked something out of the park or have made a mess of a big job. I don't let either my failures or my successes define me. That's true for you too. That's true for everybody.'

Amy looked doubtful.

'I know you said you couldn't help criticising your daughter when she was practising the piano. But you still love her the same, whether or not she bangs the wrong note out here and there. It doesn't make you think any less of her, does it?'

'No. And I knew how hard she was trying. I just had that first reaction, which I'm ashamed of. But when I take a step back I know I need to cut her some slack.'

'So why can't you do the same for yourself?'

'Well ...' She appeared stumped for a couple of seconds before she managed to pick her thread up again. 'I've got high standards. They're really important to me.'

'Good! You should be asking a lot of yourself. But you can do that without eviscerating yourself every time you don't get something quite right. Make sure you take time to celebrate the successes. Enjoy the fact that you're doing well. And when you make a mistake, don't treat it as a judgement on you. Just see it as an opportunity to learn. It's something you can use to help you get better and stronger.'

THE POWER OF PROGRESS

When I was younger I believed that the day would come when I'd have everything worked out. I'd be this god-like figure who always made the right decisions, who always did the right thing. It's only recently that I've properly come to understand that none of us will ever reach that final point. Nobody's ever going to give you a gold medal and say, 'Well done, you're now the best version of yourself.' It's a process that will go on and on and on.

But that's liberating. Because when you realise that perfection doesn't exist, and that nobody's perfect (not me, not you, not anybody), then suddenly you realise that you've got space to get things the wrong way round, or to mess up, or to (occasionally) do stupid stuff. And it doesn't mean you're unusual. It just means you're a human!

The pressure to be perfect can be a suffocating burden. But if you realise that all you can do is aim to get a little bit better each day, you'll be set free. As a society, we're really bad at recognising incremental improvements. We overlook those tiny steps forward most of us are making most of the time. And yet they're what we should be celebrating. If you've made a fraction of progress since you woke up this morning, then you're already smashing it.

RELATIVE VALUES

Just as everyone has a different definition of perfection, so everyone has their own definition of success. My triumph might be your failure. It's an entirely relative concept.

Not, of course, that you'd know this if you look at the way we're educated. As children we're invariably taught that there's a 'right way' of getting to the 'right' answer. It's a form of indoctrination that restricts our ability to think creatively. This is how you do it! But in the real world there are always so many different routes we can take, so many different solutions we can try. Life is very rarely as simple or as formulaic as an algebra problem.

But it's so hard to get a clear view of what success means to us because we're always being bombarded by other people's definitions of what it means to be successful. The point is, though, that there are plenty of doctors and CEOs who feel they are failing. Owning a Mercedes is great, but does it really prove anything about you? Or is it just a sign that you're doing a good job of meeting other people's expectations?

Life is not a competition, and the sooner you realise that, the happier you'll be. But it's hard, because the message that we are given over and over again is that our success is completely relative to other people's. Unless we're doing better than our friends or neighbours, we're not seen to be doing well at all.

The thing is, there are seven billion people on this planet. Someone is always going to be doing better than you. There will always be other human beings to compare yourself with. Somebody with a bigger house, or yacht. If you try to measure your success by those standards, you'll never feel successful. You're fighting against a relentless, unbeatable machine. It will never be satisfied, and so neither will you.

And, remember, society wants you to think like this. Because then you'll become the perfect cog in its machine, working hard doing a job you don't enjoy for a firm you don't like to buy things you don't need that won't make you happy. Society relies on you being like this. It needs you to remain on the treadmill.

I think that deep down we all know this. Our understanding of how trapped we are creeps out of the dark corners of our brain in those brief moments when we're alone and at peace. We understand how wrong all of this is. We understand how strange it is that we've exchanged the freedoms we enjoyed for thousands of years for a cramped, panicked existence at the beck and call of a system that doesn't care about us or our best interests. It's not bothered whether we're happy or sad, or fulfilled or empty; it just needs us to keep turning up for work and spending our money.

This is why it's so important to take the time to work out what real success means to you. You must be as honest with yourself as you can. Do what you can to empty your mind of all the aspirations that other people have for you, or that society expects you to hold. What do YOU want? If you were looking back on your life, would you really see success as being about having a nice car in your drive, or would it actually be the difference you were able to make to the happiness of other people?

You could live in a caravan and still be the happiest person alive. My brother Daniel's like that, and I'm so proud and happy that he's worked that out about himself. He's got that special ability to tune out all of the pressure that crushes so many others. For me, the ultimate success isn't material. You can't measure it in money in the bank or likes on Instagram. All I want is that people who meet me see me as a good person. Your view of success will be different. FIND IT.

LESSONS

- The sooner you get the idea of perfection out of your head, the better. The question we should ask ourselves isn't, 'Is it perfect?' It should be, 'Can I make it work for me?'

- It's important to set yourself high standards, but if you expect perfection from yourself you're guaranteeing you'll be unhappy. Perfection doesn't exist. Progress does. That's what you should be aiming for. That's what we should all be better at celebrating. If you're only even a little further on than you were yesterday, then you're moving in the right direction.

- If you spend your life waiting for the perfect opportunity or working away at your plan until it's perfect, you'll never get anywhere. Don't use the quest for perfection as an excuse. Get out there. Make mistakes. Create something. Because waiting built nothing.

- Our concept of perfection is relative. So is our understanding of success. Find out what success means to you, then hold on to that idea. Don't fall into the trap of judging your achievements by other people's standards.

CHAPTER 18

YOU'RE AFRAID TO STEP OUTSIDE YOUR COMFORT ZONE

I BELIEVE THAT there are two ways of thinking about comfort zones. One is the more literal sense of it as a place that you need to visit now and then, a place where you can recharge and reassess and reflect. When you're there, you can take stock of how far you've come and how far you still need to travel. It's important to remember that not everything you do inside that comfort zone should just be mindless sloth and that at least some of it should be in service of becoming the best version of yourself once you step outside it.

Home is my comfort zone. I relish the chance to completely switch off, to sit on my couch and watch shit TV. There are evenings when Emilie will want to watch a long film and I have to ask if we can give it a miss because I just don't have the brainpower to follow it. I'm very happy to carry on watching my kids' favourite cartoons long after they've gone to bed.

Once or twice a month I'll go out to the firepit I've got in my garden. The way that the flames skip and dance, never making the same shape twice, is hypnotic to me. It feels meaningful to be so close to a source of the heat and light that are so central to mankind's existence. So I'll sit entranced by the fire and watch it for an hour or so, doing little more than poking it occasionally. People who see me can sometimes get worried – I guess I must look as if I'm contemplating deep, gloomy questions. But I'm not. I'm calm and peaceful, gently shedding the accumulated stresses of whatever I've been through over the last few days until, finally, my mind is completely purged. Eventually everything I've done and achieved becomes irrelevant. Everything falls away, and the only thing that's important is who I am and what I'm feeling at that exact moment. What is the project I need to focus on *right now*? How am I going to tackle it? What do I need to ask of myself? What do I need to ask of others? I guess it offers the same thing to me as meditation does to others. I emerge 100 per cent ready to fully focus on my next task.

So it's imperative that you go to your comfort zone, and equally important that you only stay there for just enough time. I think of it like being a phone charging. You're never going to be able to get it beyond 100 per cent, no matter how long you leave it plugged in. All you're doing is wasting electricity. For me, a day, perhaps two days, is enough. Robots are designed to stay within their comfort zones. Human beings are not.

When you stay there too long, when you get *too* comfortable, you run the risk of getting into the sort of headspace where you over-analyse and over-think everything. The moment you start twitching or getting restive is the moment you need to get out of that comfort zone and return into the world again. You're fully charged now, so you need to start exuding some of that energy. Start testing yourself. Start throwing yourself into challenges. Use the energy to commit to something new, something that stretches you.

This happens to me every three months or so. When Emilie asks me why I'm pacing around the house like a caged lion, I know that it's time to change things up.

When I come back, I'm a different person. Recently, I was sitting on my couch, feeling that I need to do *something*, when my phone lit up. A text from my mate Nims. Did I want to climb K2 in three months' time? Is the pope a Catholic? I replied instantly: Yes.

Nims doesn't mess about. 'Send me your passport details now,' he told me. 'I need to sort out your visa and our climbing permits.' Bang. There was no decision to make – it had been far too long since I'd really tested myself like this. I get a buzz from *SAS: Australia*, but that was last October.

The next day, as casually as I could, I said to Emilie, 'Just to let you know, I'm climbing K2 in July.'

'That's exciting! July 2023, that should give you plenty of time to get ready.'

'No, this year.'

This is where Emilie comes into her own. 'I knew something like this was coming down the road,' she said. 'You've been far too jumpy recently. You've been like a kettle that's been on the boil for too long without anything to release the pressure. You need a vent. We all need you to have a vent.'

It was the same sense of something swelling inside me that in the past, when I lived in a different headspace, would have had me telling myself: 'I'm due a tear-up.' Now I look for a vent that I know won't be detrimental to me or the people around me. It's got to offer progression, not regression.

THE COMFORT TRAP

The other way to talk about comfort zones is as something closer to a state of mind. When you're in this state of mind you're afraid to try new things or go to new places. You're afraid of challenges, you're afraid of failure. You think that it doesn't really matter whether or not you like your life the way it is now – at least it's familiar, at least it's safe. Better the devil you know.

But, of course, this way of existing ensures that you end up trapped behind a wall. You're denying yourself any chance to grow. You might think you're happy just to flat-line. But what are you going to get out of that? A flat life.

This situation can get truly painful on those occasions when, even though you know you're stagnating, you cannot bring yourself to make the changes you know, deep down, your life needs. So you'll feel that agitation about the job you've been at for too long. You begin to resent those familiar faces, you start to fucking hate the work that you know so well you can do it with your eyes closed. And yet something keeps you strapped in, because no matter how much you wish you never have to hear that colleague's voice again, the idea of leaving this safe, comfortable environment feels even more unbearable. Why burn it all down?

All of this leads to depression, stress, sometimes even violence and aggression.

BEN HAD BUILT up a decent career for himself as an accountant. He was ticking along pretty nicely, even if there was the odd day when he found himself casting around for something to do. He told me that he was really settled in his flat, which was in a smart part of town, just a couple of roads away from where his parents still lived. He saw them a lot, as well as the same mates he'd gone to school with.

But when I met him he was wondering for the first time whether this was actually what he wanted to do for the rest of his life. The trigger for him was that the company he worked for had asked him if he'd be interested in being seconded to their Singapore office. It was supposed to be a temporary arrangement, although there was the possibility that if everyone involved agreed that it was working out, it could be turned into something more permanent.

Ben was torn. Part of him was really excited about the idea of starting again in a new city. He knew that in some ways he'd gone a bit stale in his hometown and was ready for something different. It wasn't that he was actively unhappy, but very little about his life challenged him, and even he sensed that he'd got a little too comfortable. When he talked about his routines it was like listening to a man fifty years his senior describing donning his slippers and lighting his pipe at the end of the day.

The problem was that another part of Ben was dead against any sort of change. He talked with trepidation about the challenges of moving to an unfamiliar city, one that was far bigger than anything he'd ever experienced before. He was intimidated by the prospect of having to navigate a strange culture and anxious about meeting new people. One thing that fed into his fears, he told me, was his experience at university. Ben had gone away to Manchester to study, but had got so homesick that he'd come back after just two terms. Half of him was terrified by what would happen if he stepped away from his cushy, sheltered existence, and half of him was terrified by what would happen if he didn't.

'I know what you're going to say,' he said, looking a bit sheepish as he spoke. 'You're going to tell me that I'm stuck in my comfort zone and that I need to get out. I *know* that. Everybody else knows that too. But it's one thing to say it, and it's a completely different thing to actually do it.'

'Yeah,' I replied, 'you're right, I am going to tell you that. But I've got more to say too. Look, it's absolutely normal that you should feel intimidated before doing something like this. If I'm going to be honest with you, as excited as I felt before climbing Everest, I was also pretty overwhelmed. I was confident in my own abilities, but that didn't mean that I wasn't also anxious about the sheer scale of the task. I mean, climbing to the top of the world is the literal definition of stepping outside your comfort zone.

'But what I realised then is that my body was telling me that what I was about to face mattered to me. You should try to see that feeling as a positive, a sign that you're heading in the right direction. Because a life lived without ever experiencing that feeling might seem safe and comfortable, but it's going to remain small. And so, unfortunately, are you.'

'I get that,' he said, 'I really do. But it's all so much at once. I think I'll be overwhelmed. And I'm worried that if I go out and make a mess of things, or just hate it so much I want to get straight back on the plane and fly home, it'll be like my time in Manchester again. Except this time, I'll be so scarred that I'll never want to try anything new again. Maybe I should pass on this one, and wait for something that's a bit easier to digest.'

'You could do that,' I replied, 'but I think you'll be waiting a fucking long time for the "right" opportunity, because I think that there's a big enough part of you that's so afraid of leaving your comfort zone that nothing that ever comes your way will ever seem like the "right opportunity". The attitude I have with anything like this is: I'll deal with whatever comes my way. There's no reason why the very same should not be true for you. There are so many things that you do now and take for granted that would once have scared the shit out of you.

'I bet you no longer give riding your bike a second thought. It's almost as natural as walking. But there would have been a time when you never would have thought it was possible to ride it without stabilisers. You stepped way outside your comfort zone then. You can do it again now. Just take that first step. One single step. Say yes. Get on that plane, and then when something comes up that you find uncomfortable, like the language barrier, deal with it. One little problem at a time.'

Reader, he got on that plane.

THE JOY OF BLINDNESS

Many people are like Ben – they're reluctant to leave their comfort zone because they're afraid of the unknown. But you're never going to have perfect knowledge of the future. The only way you'll ever find out what's going to happen is either to commit, take the plunge and soak up the consequences whatever they may be, or do nothing and live with regret, because once again life has rushed past and left you behind.

The thing is, I'm not afraid of what I don't know. I'm excited by it. There's nothing more exciting to me than walking into a room and having no idea what's going to happen next. Because these are the situations in which you have to engage your brain, feelings and energy. This is how you learn – by jumping into the unknown. When you enter a familiar space, your mind and body aren't engaged in the same way. I feel so bored when I know where I'm going, what I'm doing, what I'm going to say.

That's not to say you need to dedicate your entire life to the search for the unknown or unexpected. What's important is that you should never let yourself be trapped by a fear of what you don't know. Because if you leave the wall standing, you'll be left with the nagging question: what's behind it? What could I have become? Those regrets are going to eat away at your mind. They'll for ever be pulling at you.

You don't need to demolish the whole thing in one go – just remove a few bricks. Each brick is another small commitment. Before you know it, you'll have created a doorway. It might be that you then want to stride right through. Or perhaps you'll take a look, and then conclude that you're just not ready yet. Or maybe you'll put all those bricks back. But at least you know what's there now.

THE EDGE

Your ability to make the necessary move is always going to depend upon how much self-belief you have. But, of course, you can increase that self-belief by ensuring you're constantly stepping out of your comfort zone.

What's important to understand is that stepping outside your comfort zone isn't just about leaping out of helicopters or confronting your fear of snakes by letting a zookeeper drape a python around your neck. It can also be small, almost inconsequential things. It can be something as seemingly unimportant as taking a slightly different route to work, or making that slightly complex phone call you've been putting off for a while.

You only need to do things that are just on the edge of what you find comfortable. If you're exposing yourself to new sights, sounds and experiences, you're taking yourself outside your comfort zone. You're asking your body and mind to respond to these unfamiliar environments. You're making them work. So that's why I try to spend more time outside my comfort zone than inside it. I'm constantly doing things to make myself uncomfortable, physically, mentally, socially and professionally. I deliberately put myself into situations where I know I'm going to struggle, or fail.

It's also why when I talk to people who have agoraphobia, I don't tell them to throw themselves immediately into a heaving crowd of people. I just ask them to step outside their porch, even if it's just for a few seconds, then to go back inside and close the door behind them. Sit down for a minute or two, collect themselves. When they feel ready to go a bit further, I suggest that they might take a few steps down the driveway.

The only way you're going to find out who you really are and what you're capable of is by going out there and witnessing the world. Use your eyes, use your ears. Talk to people. Make mistakes. Most of us don't appreciate the psychological benefits brought by doing something that's apparently so simple. Action sets your neurons firing. It lights your mind up.

Put one foot in front of another. When you do this, your mind is making hundreds, thousands, of micro-decisions. How much energy do you need to push off from your standing leg. Where do you place your shoe, what angle should the sole meet the gravel, how much force do you need to use? Then you start walking up a slight incline. The decisions continue to flow. Doing stuff that goes against the grain of what everybody else is doing, even in tiny ways, can make a big difference. It stops you feeling as if you're part of the ant farm. And it becomes addictive. When you're walking like this, you're free.

Or, if you head out and start socialising, you're giving your brain another sort of workout. You're asking it to empathise with others, to try to work out what they're thinking and how you should respond. You're forcing it to collect and process vast streams of data.

If your response to that is, 'Oh, I don't like crowds, or new people, I'll lock myself away,' then you're going to struggle. You don't realise the good that all of this is doing you.

The more your mind is working, the more psychologically stimulated you become, the more problems you solve, the more solutions you come up with. You begin to think once more, 'I can. I am capable.'

EXERCISE

Try to get into the habit of finding solutions to tricky situations that would normally lie outside your comfort zone.
Think about what you would do if …

- Your car gets a puncture while you're driving to a doctor's appointment.
- You need to confront a bully who is a teammate at your local rugby club.
- Your boss asks you to go on a work trip with colleagues you've never met before.

NO HALF-MEASURES

The military used to be like the biggest boys' club in the world. While you were in it, you felt untouchable. The SBS gave me the licence to do pretty much whatever I wanted. The authority it gave me was addictive. For a while.

But I eventually became bored of what I was doing and increasingly intrigued about what was coming next. I kept on thinking: where do I go from here? And one thought wouldn't go away: I need to do something else. I realised I didn't care about promotions, most of all because I was fairly sure the next step for me would be becoming an ops officer, which would have meant working behind a desk. I'd been a point man, a primary fires operator and a team leader. So I knew that I was done there. But I was still really young.

The only route for me was to take a leap into a completely different environment.

Some breaks, however, are not quite as clear-cut as they seem. Although I was sure that I didn't belong in the military anymore – and I never regretted leaving – it still took me many years to actually accept that I was no longer a soldier. The profession of arms still had a hold over much of my consciousness and imagination. I continued to dream I was in uniform. I was half-in, half-out.

The military had been such a defining part of my identity. It had been so important to me to be seen as an elite soldier.

I'd always relished that tiny shiver of recognition other soldiers gave you when they saw you cutting around the base. So much of my self-worth depended on these external validations.

But this ambiguity was holding me back. I was getting zero benefit from keeping a foot in each camp. In fact, I was probably getting the worst of both worlds. It holds you back on every level: financially, emotionally, psychologically. It arrests your capacity for growth. Half of you is always going to remain dormant.

That's what I'll always say to ex-military guys who want to make a go of civvy street. 'Cut away that military demeanour.' That's not saying that you should abandon your mates. Far from it. But you do have to change the way you engage with the world.

When you join a business, immerse yourself fully in it, give it 100 per cent of yourself. Keep doing that until you have a solid foundation. When you've got that, you can take the odd step back into your old life, because by then you know you won't be drawn into it again. It's a bit like marriage – it isn't going to work if you're always thinking about, or talking to, your ex.

BOTTOM RUNG

You need to have the courage to start at the bottom of the ladder all over again. That's a problem a lot of people encounter. They don't want to try new things because they don't want to have to work their way up once more. They're afraid of not knowing everything; they're afraid of the inevitable loss of status.

What they forget, however, is that they already have a head start. Think of all the knowledge and experience you've accumulated. When I switched from being a soldier to a TV personality I was entering a world about which I knew pretty much nothing. I had no idea of the technical requirements. I knew sweet FA about camera angles or the production process. But I was an experienced leader of men. I was aware of my charisma. I knew how to get along with people.

REMEMBER *WHY* YOU'RE DOING THIS

Some people step out of their comfort zone, and because they don't achieve their immediate goals they think they've failed, so they don't do it again. Others make that step, achieve what they set out to do, and promptly decide that they never need to do anything so foolish ever again. Both approaches miss the point.

I hesitate to use the word, because it's become such a cliché, but here it is. It's all about the journey. It's about collecting those moments in time, the things that have actually happened, not the could-haves, the would-haves and the should-haves, but tangible experiences.

LESSONS

- We all need time to rest, recuperate and take stock of where our life's at. It's really important that we do this. But it's also really important that we don't stay in our comfort zone any longer than necessary.

- A lot of the time people don't understand why they get snappy or start feeling uncomfortable within themselves, even though they've been relaxing. It's their body and mind telling them it's time to get moving!

- I don't see leaving my comfort zone as a negative experience that needs to be endured. For me, it's a positive experience to be embraced. Because it's when you leave your comfort zone that life gets really exciting. It's the fastest way to learn and grow.

- Once you've made that first step out of your comfort zone, when you realise you can do it and have seen the benefits it brings, you'll never want to stop. Try to maintain a permanent sense of momentum. Otherwise, when you get stuck, as you definitely will at some point, the idea of moving at all might appear so much harder than it needs to be.

- You don't always need to be making huge leaps outside your comfort zone. You just need to explore the outer edge of what you're comfortable with. Do enough to get your brain working, and then go a tiny bit further next time.

- There will be times when leaving your comfort zone will involve a big change in your life. When you do this, you must leave your past behind and commit fully to whatever it is you've chosen for your future. If your head is in two places at once, it's not really anywhere at all.

CHAPTER 19

YOU WANT TO CHANGE BUT YOU DON'T KNOW HOW

MY PHOBIA IS being stuck in a small space, unable to move. This explains a lot about the way my life has turned out. I need room to grow. I need the freedom to roam and find out who I really am.

It was only the other day that I was thinking how much I've changed over the years. I've gone from the shy teenage recruit who could barely meet anybody's eye as I walked into the barracks for the first time to the man I am now. I'm a family man. I'm empathetic. But if I'm confident now, it's only the result of a long, hard journey.

At times, especially when I was younger, I changed because I had to. But more and more, I've changed because I *want* to. I've embraced the idea that we're all a dynamic work-in-progress, that we should all be looking to change and grow. And that this is a process that's not going to stop until the day we take our last breath. I want to still be evolving even when every hair on my head has turned white.

Being in the military restricted who I was. For a while it made me think that drinking myself into oblivion was an excellent idea. It even persuaded me that drinking warm piss out of a tatty desert boot would make others respect me. I thought that joining the Special Forces would help calm me down. It didn't. Or, at least, it didn't do enough to calm me down. I was still spending all my wages on going out, three or four bottles of champagne in one evening, at £300 a pop.

Then I left the military, and walked into an almost ready-made persona as a scrapper and a hardman. It took too long for me to realise that there was a huge gap between this persona and who I really was. Or, to be more accurate, who I wanted to be. I realised then that I'm supposed to be around people. I get a buzz off other human beings. I want to help them. I'm truly not the slightest bit interested in trying to smash their faces in.

I needed prison to give me the excuse I'd been looking for to say, 'I'm not a fighter anymore. I'm not a drinker anymore.' It meant I could walk away from a brawl and people would go, 'Yeah, of course, he doesn't want to go back to jail.' I could shed the skin of the person I'd probably never really been. What a fucking relief.

I think for me, the next stage is leaving behind as completely as I can the persona of the chief instructor. You might find it hard to believe, but I detest having to scream and shout at people. Although I'm still trying to do it to achieve a positive outcome, I'm using a persona that I outgrew many years ago. Whenever I'm on set, I'm stepping back into a mindset that in all other areas of my life I've left behind. I think that's why I often return home completely exhausted from filming the show. It's so tiring pretending to be somebody that doesn't exist anymore. I want you to see me as I really am – the caring, empathetic father – not the caricature that the media sometimes shows you.

But I also know that I'm lucky that my story got that twist. An event came along that gave me the permission I'd been waiting for to change. I don't want you to have to hit rock bottom before you realise you're allowed to be a different person. What I want you to understand is that there's no need to wait for that permission, like I did. You shouldn't need anybody else to tell you that it's OK to change. If you want to change, then you need to do it. It's as simple as that. If that desire to be different is already inside you, why delay a second longer than you need to?

THE RESTLESS GENE

We're designed to change. We're designed to evolve. Nothing's ever permanent as we're actually in a continual state of flux. That's who we are! Ninety-eight per cent of the atoms in our bodies change every single year. And you're reading this book right now because of mankind's innate restlessness, its inbuilt desire to try new things, go to new places.

We're here in Europe because roughly a hundred thousand years ago in Africa a member of our species said, 'Let's just see what's over there.' They committed to that decision. Once they did that, they confronted, and solved, all the problems involved with getting 'over there'.

The trick is to recognise that we all have this restless gene and to harness its energy – to recognise it as an opportunity, not a curse. Unfortunately, too often we fight against it – the most natural process there is.

I can understand why: change is rarely comfortable. That's as true of finding a new relationship as it is of finding a new job or making a profound change to your lifestyle. But I think that when something is difficult, it's usually a sign that it's also worthwhile. You can't make a sustainable diet out of low-hanging fruit.

IMPOSTER SYNDROME

Change can very often be bewildering or unsettling. It can take a little while to accustom ourselves to the new person we've become or the new environment we've begun to inhabit. And it's often in these moments of adjustment and acclimatisation that imposter syndrome can strike.

Imposter syndrome hinders our capacity to change. It can be the thing that stops us from trying new things that in our heart of hearts we know we need to do, because other people are trying to persuade us that we're not good enough, that we don't deserve the life we've worked so hard for. The worst thing is, we internalise it. In our head we start to repeat their negative words and after a while we begin to believe them. We become our own worst enemies. We finish the work that others have started.

I get it all the time and have to fight hard against it. 'How can he be a mental health advocate?' 'Why does he think he has the right to talk about positivity?' And on, and on, and fucking on.

Change is natural, so when imposter syndrome forces people to suppress that impulse – when they tell themselves, 'Somebody like me could never be a doctor' or 'How dare I aim to become a CEO?' – it creates terrible friction.

You should never fall into the trap of thinking that you're one single thing and that's how you're going to be for ever. This is as true of positive labels as it is negative ones. If I defined myself for ever as the person who had climbed Mount Everest, it would be just as restrictive as if I only saw myself as a man who'd been shut away in prison.

Don't let who you are now strangle all the people you *could* become in the future.

YOU'RE A GOOD BOY, YOU'RE NOT GOING TO CHANGE

When somebody says to you, 'Never change who you are, fella. You're a good boy, you're not going to change,' then what they're really trying to do is force you to stay in the box they think you belong in. The idea that you might want to escape that box and live a different, bigger existence than the one they've assigned you shits them up.

When I hear that I get a chill running down my spine. I think, 'If I *don't* change, if I stand still, I'm going to be just like you. I'm going to be like 98 per cent of the world.' That's not something I can live with. I'm like a shark. These animals have to keep moving – if they stop, they die. I know that if I'm not changing, I'm not learning and I'll quickly become stagnant, stuck in the void.

I had that with the military. There was a sizeable group of people who couldn't get beyond one single idea: 'Once a Marine, always a Marine.' In their minds, everything I did after leaving uniform was make-believe. As they saw it, I was just pretending to be an author, or a media figure, or a businessman. Sooner or later, they thought, reality would strike. I'd see I'd got above myself and retreat back to my true existence. 'How can you go from hardcore tours of Afghanistan to designing clothes?'

They weren't bad people. They just couldn't accept that I

had a sincere desire to become a different sort of human being. What they saw as me getting above my station was really just me moving forward.

I was reminded of that experience during a conversation with a man called Simon after one of my recent speaking tours. He was a lad who was out every weekend drinking, and very often he'd get into a scrap. Then he'd wake up on Sunday morning with a crashing hangover and completely skint, and he'd ask himself, 'What the fuck did I do last night?' As he was describing his lifestyle, I had an almost uncanny feeling: it was as if I were talking to the person I'd been a decade or so ago.

The thing is, he was desperate to change, but he couldn't find a way to break away from that cycle. Inside he was saying to himself, 'I really don't want to be doing this anymore,' but he'd gained a kind of reputation and was struggling to shake it off. He was trapped by his notoriety. Every time he'd tried to take even a small step back from the endless nights of booze and punch-ups, there'd be a stream of messages from his friends asking him why he'd stayed at home: 'Stop being so boring,' 'Why are you such a pussy?' Before long these messages would have their effect and he'd be out on the razz again. He was repressing the better part of himself so that he could fit into the shape that others wanted him to be.

It was weird, he told me, but he felt that if he changed it would be as if he were letting his mates down. He was also afraid of what they'd say.

I had one word for him: 'Change.'

He looked at me blankly. I stared back.

'It's too hard,' he said.

'I know. But you've got to do it. You've got to take that leap. If you want to escape, you've got to make a drastic change. When it was my time to do that, I cut my entire circle out. For five years I didn't go out. I realised that if I couldn't look after the people inside my family, then it was madness to keep on trying to help the people outside it. And yeah, of course, to begin with there was the chorus of complaining text messages and the like. All that achieved was that it showed me really clearly who I didn't need in my life.

'If you're fed up with feeling like shit when you wake up,' I continued, 'then drink less. Better still, don't put yourself in those situations. Why not do something else? You're spending £200 every weekend on getting out of your head. Why not put petrol in your car and take your family out into the countryside? If you've not got a family, why not go on a cycling trip or get into climbing? The people you think are your mates will fall away. And all the time you'll be getting fitter and psychologically more robust.'

EXERCISE

- Who do you want to be?
- Write down the qualities you want to embody.
- What steps can you take to embody them?
- What can you do to actually *live* these values rather than just talk about them?

NO GOING BACK

'It's got to be a drastic change,' I told Simon. 'Half-measures don't work.'

You can't just pretend to change and hope that somehow the world will rearrange itself around you to suit your needs. You do have to actually change. But the thing about change is that it's super-hard. There will be stigma. You're going to get judged. People will talk all kinds of shit about you.

So you'll need to keep implementing that change until everybody around you gets the message. They need to understand that it isn't just a phase or a flight of fancy. This is who you've become. There's no going back.

I'm not going to pretend it's not hard to just shrug off those morons who are like, 'Waaaay, why aren't you drunk?' So you have to show them in the clearest terms you can that you're no longer like them. If you have two week-ends where you resist temptation and pressure and stay in, and on the third you're back out on the piss, then what message are you sending out? That you're still a knobhead, like all your mates? You've got to see it through. You're not going to alter people's perceptions in a fortnight. It might take four or five weeks for you to prove to others – and yourself – that you're serious. It might take four or five months. That drastic change must become the norm. Everybody has got to become used to it.

Discipline is key, as it will help you break the problem's back. Emotional intelligence is important too. Pay attention to your emotions, try to work out exactly what you're feeling and why. When the urge to go out strikes you – and it probably will – don't give in, and don't ignore it.

Find a motivator. It might be as simple as feeling better physically. If a month passes without you going out on the lash, you'll inevitably discover that you've lost weight and have more energy. You'll probably feel happier in yourself and you won't be subject to mood swings. So, although being disciplined sucks, the *results* of that discipline can make all the difference.

And don't focus too much on what you're going to lose by changing your lifestyle. Instead, try to think more about what you're about to gain. Wouldn't it be better to be fully present as you watch your kid take their first steps or successfully ride a bike for the first time? Wouldn't you rather be able to say to yourself: 'I saw that! I saw my child pedalling across our front yard!'

What can also be really useful is finding someone to talk to who understands who you are and what you're trying to do. Stay away from your old drinking buddies and seek out one of your half-sensible mates instead, or a family member or colleague. When you've got someone like that to confide in, it makes it so much easier to resist all the temptation and peer pressure.

And always, always, remember how important it is to be honest with yourself. If you've cheated on your partner, then you'll know that you're not behaving like the person you want to be. The fact that you claim you prefer to go to the gym or read than go out drinking is irrelevant if that's not what you actually do. If you get smashed every Friday and Saturday, then that's who you *are*.

THE HARDEST WORD IN THE WORLD

The hardest word to say in the world is 'no', but I reckon I've got to the point now when most people are actually surprised when I say 'yes'. There was a time when I was so desperate to please that I agreed to everything. If you'd looked up 'yes-man' in the dictionary, you'd have found my name. That couldn't last.

Not 'yes', not 'perhaps', not 'maybe'. You've got to learn the power of the word 'no'. It's a lot better to be honest and give a decisive no. If you just claim that you can't go out on the lash because you're ill, or busy, or just don't fancy it tonight but maybe next week, then you're not demonstrating to anybody that you've made any kind of meaningful change in your life. Once you start saying no, once you've stuck with it, you'll be showing the world that you've broken the cycle.

So just try saying no once. Prove to yourself that you can do it. Then do it again, and again, and again. There's no quicker way to take charge of your own life.

CHANGING TRIBES

Work and family will always make their claims on your time, but you should be in charge of all of the hours that are left over. What are you going to do with that time? Who are you going to spend it with? With the best will in the world, we all only have limited stocks of energy and positivity. If you're going to invest the best of yourself in a bunch of wasters, then you don't need the brains of a particle physicist to work out what you're going to become. A fucking waster.

At the end of the day we all want to belong to something. We don't want to be alone on this earth. This sense of belonging can come from our partner, our children, our wider family or friends. Sometimes people get it from sports teams. But occasionally we want to belong so much that we'll suppress who we really are.

But your tribe will inevitably change. For a long time I got my sense of belonging from the military. It was such a huge part of my identity. It affected the way I behaved and dressed, even the way I spoke. And I was willing to let all that happen just so I belonged. Now my family and business partners are my tribe. Once I relied on soldiers to have my back, but they're not there anymore. Instead, I know that if anything happens to me I'll always be able to fall back on Emilie, or Jez and Arf. The thing is, it's not like renewing your home insurance; you're never going to get a letter telling you that it's time to start hanging out with different people. That's up to you.

The change happens when you realise that you no longer want to waste those precious resources on negative people or environments. The core of who you are doesn't need to change. If you're an empathetic, driven, positive individual, that's a constant; it's ingrained in you. What does need to be transformed are the places where you put your empathy, your drive, your positivity.

That's what's happened to me. I've been stung too many times. I've lent money to people who I know deep down are never going to pay it back. So although I've not stopped being empathetic, I've just chosen to point my empathy in a different direction.

LESSONS

- If there's a gap between the person you want to be, and the person you actually are in your day-to-day life, then I guarantee you'll be unhappy. It's up to you to make the change needed to close that gap.

- Don't be like how I once was. Don't sit there waiting for an excuse to change. If you want to change, if you feel you *need* to change, then that's the only permission you need.

- Time is precious. So be careful how you dish it out and who you dish it out to.

- We've all got to satisfy our need to belong. We all search continually for a place we can call home, in the widest sense. There will be times in our lives when we find that sense of belonging. But the attraction that these people and places exert upon us does not remain constant. The club that felt like home one year might not feel quite so comfortable the next. Be prepared to change your tribe.

- When people start slagging you off behind your back, shaking their heads and saying that you've 'changed', then you should be pleased. They're proving your point. They're showing you exactly why you needed to evolve.

THE HAMMER

SO THAT'S IT. I've no more advice to give, no more stories to tell. It's all up to you now. Do you want to be a people-pleaser or the master of your own destiny? Do you want to spend your life trapped by fears about what others might think, or do you want to be able to stride into the future unburdened by anxiety? Do you want to waste your life in a futile search for perfection, or do you want to take positive steps towards addressing your deepest-rooted problems? Do you want to be the sort of person whose progress is stunted because they cannot locate the motivation they need, or do you want to steadily build your self-belief until nothing seems impossible anymore. Do you want to remain the person you are, right now, or do you want to commit to a life of permanent change, permanent progress?

All of this is in your hands. You should know that I've got absolute faith in you. You're so much stronger and more capable than you think. You just need to realise that. I hope that this book will help you on that journey. I want you to see it as a tool. How you use it is of course your call. But I like to see it as the hammer that will help you smash through whatever walls have come to stand between you and your potential.

As I've written this book I've been inspired by the stories of people from across the country who've shared with me their own experiences of courageously confronting the challenges they've faced. I'd love it if, next time I write a book, one of the stories that inspires me is yours.

ACKNOWLEDGEMENTS

I CAME TO books later in life. I had to smash through my own reading wall to connect with them, but writing has given me huge amounts of satisfaction. My books are an important part of my life now – they're part of who I am, and they wouldn't happen without you, my readers. I take nothing for granted and appreciate every read, listen, repost and like. Thank you.

Thanks must also go the excellent publishing team that helps me get my words down on the page and this book into your hands. Thank you to Josh Ireland for bringing so much to this project – you smashed it again. Thank you to my team at HarperCollins: Adam Humphrey, Orlando Mowbray, Simon Armstrong, Alan Cracknell, Simon Gerratt, Claire Ward, Tom Dunstan, Caroline Bovey, Alice Gomer and Hannah Avery. You deliver for me every time.

Thanks to my management team: my man Jordan Johnson, Lizzie Barroll Brown, Mary Bekhait and everyone at YMU. Thanks also to Amanda Harris, my literary agent, who is as ambitious for my books as I am. Let's keep the bestsellers coming, Amanda!

To my brothers Michael Middleton, Mike Morris, Jez, brother Arf, brother Paddy (Damien) and my Uncle Andy. My ultimate team! Each one of you has a direct positive impact in my life. Terry, thanks for being on it, Cus 🙏

Most importantly, and for always, thanks and love go to my amazing wife Emilie and my beautiful children Oakley, Shyla, Gabriel, Priseïs and Bligh.